Eat Right,
Train Right

Thank you so much to Himla for lending us linen tablecloths, to Iittala for lending us beautiful porcelain, and to the grocery stores Aubergine and Cajsa Warg in the Södermalm district of Stockholm, where we took some of the photos.

www.skyhorsepublishing.com

10 9 8 7 6 5 4 3 2 1
Library of Congress Cataloging-in-Publication Data is available on file.
ISBN: 978-1-62087-728-9
Printed in China
Interior design by Anna Hild

RECIPES
THAT YIELD
RESULTS!

Eat Right, Train Right

Nutritious Recipes to Lose Weight, Build Muscle, and Get Fit

Niclas Ericsson
Camilla Porsman Reimhult

Photography by Christian Hagward

Translation by Monika Romare

Skyhorse Publishing

Using the Nutritional Tables

We have calculated the nutritional values for the recipes in this book so that you can easily select a serving size that meets your energy needs, and lives up to your workout goals. The color symbols in the nutritional tables for each recipe should be read as follows:

⬤ = Entire Batch

⬤ = Serving Size for Weight Lifting

⬤ = Serving Size for Endurance Training

⬤ = Serving Size for Muscle Building

⬤ = Serving Size for Weight Loss

You can read about how the portion sizes are calculated on page 28–30.

In some cases, the main ingredient will affect the serving size—especially when you are cooking a single serving as opposed to the entire batch. A salmon fillet will vary in weight depending on its size, and it is neither practical nor economical to cut away pieces to make it weigh exactly as much as the recipe calls for. In those cases, the nutritional table shows the nutritional value for the entire portion, depending on the serving of salmon: 3.5 oz (100 g), 5.3 oz (150 g), 7 oz (200 g), and so on.

The basic idea behind this book is that you combine a source of protein with a flavor addition, a carbohydrate dish, and a vegetable dish. However, sometimes you may want to keep it simple and serve rice, pasta, or some other source of carbohydrates straight out of the packaging to save time. On page 30, you will find a table of standard serving sizes of various carbohydrate foods and their nutritional value. This will help you keep track of your energy and nutritional intake for various situations.

Table of Contents

There have been many different diet trends over the past few years. Paleolithic, Atkins, Glycemic Index diet, and the Low Carb, High Fat diet to name a few. Sometimes, it seems that different diet experts agree with each other, while at other times they appear to contradict each other. With all the mixed messages out there, it is easy to get confused when choosing your diet.

This book is here to make your life easier and to help you find a diet that suits you, whether you are doing strength training, are trying to lose weight, or are about to participate in your first marathon. We have taken into account well-established facts within nutrition physiology, and we have collected some of the information that all the diets have in common, such as the benefits of healthy fats and the effects of slow-release carbohydrates.

The recipes in this book are simple, and there are numerous ways to combine them to create variety. We have

included basic techniques that are helpful in the kitchen when you plan, shop, and prepare your lunch boxes for the week. You will find a summary of our philosophy on the next page.

The Diet Should Yield Maximum Results

If you are a exercising a lot, it may seem impossible to get enough vitamins, minerals, and protein from your diet. A lot of people even find dietary supplements necessary. That is a myth. Food that is packed with nutrients—a lot of nutrients per calorie—and balanced meals are all you need. The serving sizes are adjusted to your exercise needs so that you get the right proportions of various nutrients, no matter what your work-out goal may be.

Food Should Be Healthy

If you are exercising, you are probably very particular in ensuring that the food you eat is healthy. Not only do you need to meet your body's energy requirement, but you also need to get the other nutritional values right: the GI-value, fats, fiber content, and high-value protein. Our recipes already have all these things figured out so that you can enjoy each meal with maximum benefits. The recipes are divided into protein sources, carbohydrate sources, vegetables, and flavor additions, allowing you to easily throw together meals according to popular diets, such as GI or LCHF, or you can leave out the meat for a vegetarian dish.

Food Should be Varied and Exciting

"Workout food" tends to be boring and bland—usually staple foods that you have to cook repeatedly to stay within the boundaries of what you think you "should" be eating. However, eating the same foods over and over without any variation can lead to an unbalanced diet that will have a negative impact on your workout results. Therefore, the basic idea behind *Eat Right, Train Right* was to create recipes that can be combined in many different ways to help you create a balanced diet with lots of variety.

The photographs in this book give you ideas of especially successful combinations. You can experiment, and come up with your own favorites. We have incorporated exotic flavors from all over the world, such as tamarind, fresh turmeric, fennel seeds, and *kimchi*.

Meals Should Be Easy to Prepare

We imagine that you would rather spend your time at the gym, or out on the running track, than in front of the stove. However, an active lifestyle does not mean that you need to live on highly processed foods or fast food. All the meals in this book are easy to prepare, and you'll get plenty of tips that will ease the cooking process if you are not used to spending time in the kitchen. We give you ideas on how to express-cook foods, such as steaming vegetables in the microwave. They will be even tastier than when you cook them the traditional way—we can assure you.

Food Should Be Affordable

It can be difficult to make money last when aiming to eat healthy, especially since you need larger portions when exercising a lot. We would like you to get as much nutritional value for your money as possible, so the recipes are based on produce that can be found at regular grocery stores. In addition, we give you suggestions on how to use leftovers. Less waste is also a better choice for the environment.

Food Should Be Enjoyed, Without Guilt

We believe that each meal should give you a moment of pleasure, not feelings of guilt. Eating something less healthy than the rest of your diet every once in a while won't make you sick and obese. At least not if your diet is balanced, and well proportioned. Homemade hummus is incredibly delicious—we teach you how to make it—however, it isn't the end of the world if you pick it up at the grocery store to save time.

Feelings of guilt lead to stress, and stress will negatively affect your workout results. *Eat Right, Train Right* will help you achieve better results, and invigorate your quality of life through the joy of food, *sans* guilt.

Who Are We?

We met while studying to become personal trainers, so physical exercise is one of our mutual passions. We are journalists, and authors, but we cover different areas. Niclas is the one with the cooking talent. He has lived in Italy, France, and Rwanda, and traveled pretty much all over the world. His travels have given him inspiration for many exotic flavor ideas. How do you make cabbage exciting? How do you make bulgur interesting? How do you quickly throw together lunch boxes out of the week's leftovers? Or how do you use a mango if it isn't ripe when you cut it up? Well, Niclas knows the answers.

Give Niclas a basket of fresh produce, and he will miraculously whip up an exciting meal that you've never tasted before. Usually, it is a dish that is beneficial for your exercise needs, but that tastes like a party meal in the middle of the week. All of this happens with a few basic techniques that shorten your cooking time.

Camilla has a background in nutrition, and several instructor courses under her belt. She knows how to balance meals so that they yield maximum exercise results. Through the years, she has responded to hundreds of questions about what, and how much, to eat to facilitate the fitness journey in *Fitness Magazine,* ToppHälsa, and *Stadium Magazine.* In this book, she shares her best tips.

Camilla has chosen the healthiest and most nutrition-packed produce, and Niclas has created his recipes based on her selections.

We hope that this book will help you reach your workout goals and discover new, exciting flavor sensations.

Plan Your Success

You have a fitness goal, and you want the food you eat to help you reach that goal. Excellent.

Turning your intentions into reality requires a little bit of planning, patience, and technique. Just like your fitness routine.

Planning

People who act before they think tend to encounter unexpected problems. Imagine coming home from work, or the gym, feeling tired and hungry and on the verge of panic. Now, imagine having to think about what ingredients to use, and then having to cook the meal—that may seem overwhelming in that tired state of mind. Most likely, this type of scenario would end with the simplest possible solution, whether reaching for a protein shake, or ordering a pizza.

When you begin your new food routine, make it a habit to always have at least one nutritious meal in the house. If you own a freezer, and a microwave to defrost the frozen produce, it is very easy to store fish, chicken, octopus, or other meat in the freezer. If you don't have a freezer and a microwave, you will have to put some more thought into your planning process. Keep a few variations of rice, bulgur, quinoa, beans, and pasta at home. That will secure your source of good carbohydrates. Delicious flavor additions such as olives, anchovies, tahini, ajvar relish, soy sauce, fish sauce, or chili sauce pretty much never expire, and will be waiting for you in the fridge when your appetite strikes. Fresh produce such as eggs, plain yogurt, onion, garlic, ginger, Parmesan, lime, lemon, root vegetables such as carrots and beets, white cabbage, red cabbage, and savoy cabbage will stay fresh for a while if you store them in the fridge.

You don't need to stock the fridge with all these items simultaneously, but keep at least a few of them on hand so that you can quickly throw together a delicious and nutritious meal anytime. Just pick up a piece of salmon, or chicken, and perhaps a tasty vegetable, then look up a recipe in this book that will teach you how to cook it in no time. In addition, we give you advice on how to vary the meals. For your convenience, we have included some "panic recipes" for cooking salmon, Atlantic herring, pork tenderloin, and vegetables that pretty much cook themselves in the microwave in just a few minutes. You'll find them in the recipe index under "microwave."

Make it a habit to remember approximately what foods you have at home. It is a lot simpler than it sounds, especially if you cook on a regular basis. A simple trick: open the fridge before you leave your house each morning and take a quick peek. Or use your camera phone to capture an image of the contents of your fridge. That way you will avoid standing dumbfounded at the grocery store, wondering if you have any onions at home.

One way to create effective food habits is to set some time aside each week for shopping and cooking. Divide the time up if you want. Perhaps one hour on Saturday for important grocery runs, and two hours on Monday to cook for the entire week. If you prepare a roast beef, two pounds of *gravlax*, and two pounds of chicken fillets, you will save a lot of time during the week. Or why not prepare all three options? You won't need more than an hour of really efficient kitchen work.

Preparing vegetables or risotto will be much easier, and more fun, if you don't need to start from scratch every day. If you can complete the basic grocery run for the week and then pick up little things on your way home, the process won't feel so laborious.

If you want to give your new food habits a speedy start, you can follow one of our weekly schedules, which are already adjusted according to your workout goals, including the grocery list of what to buy. You will find the weekly schedules on www.matforresultat.se. There, you will also get more useful tips on food and exercise.

Grocery Shopping

Divide your grocery runs into dry foods/conserves, spices/flavorings, and fresh/frozen produce such as meat, fish, and vegetables. Dry foods and conserves have a shelf life that often lasts over several years. Make sure to clean out your pantry first, so that you'll have room for your new basics. It will save you plenty of time and money, because a last-minute solution is almost always an expensive option. Invest some money to stock up on different types of rice, bulgur, quinoa, and canned beans. Even if you don't use them up during the first month, you'll eventually make good use of them. Varying your carbs will make your meals more interesting.

Our recipes only call for canned goods occasionally. This is a conscious decision because fresh produce is healthier and tastier than anything that comes in a can. However, there is no reason to get worked up if you don't have the fresh alternative at hand. Keeping a few cans of anchovies, mackerel, and tuna at home is a great way to always be prepared to make a snack, or a meal that you can serve with Tart Black Quinoa (page 142) or a Hearty Wheat Berry Salad (page 136) if you happen to have some left over from the week.

Spices and flavor alternatives usually hold up for a long time. However, compared to the dried and canned foods, some of the spices and flavors used in the recipes of this book are somewhat exotic. So it may be difficult to find them at regular grocery stores.

Plan a visit to an Asian grocery store to stock up on tamarind, fresh turmeric, Szechuan pepper, black bean sauce, and *kimchi* base. Asian food shops exist in most medium sized cities today, but you can even find them in many smaller towns. These products are inexpensive, and you will only need to buy them a few times a year, since most of the ingredients have a long shelf life and are used in small quantities. Being able to vary the flavor of the produce that you tend to eat often is worth the world. You can turn a bland meal with carrots, white cabbage, salmon, or pork loin into an exciting food experience.

While you are at it, buy fish sauce, tahini, soy sauce, or Chinese chili sauce. Nowadays, you can find these products in pretty much any grocery store, but they are usually less expensive and of higher quality at an Asian food market. There, you can also find black rice and authentic sushi rice.

When it comes to fresh produce, you will need to shop a little bit more often. Count on about three times a week if you live by the philosophy of this book, and cook large batches of fish or meat a few times a week. Root vegetables, such as carrots, beets, parsnip, and different types of onions and cabbage can be stored in the fridge for a few weeks. Many other vegetables are more fragile: tomatoes, spinach, and zucchini. You should buy them when you intend to use them.

If you have access to a freezer, stock up on frozen produce. You can also freeze produce yourself, especially if you happen to find a good deal on a big package of salmon, chicken, pork tenderloin, or any other good basics. They are great to keep at home, and the quality won't change much during the freezing process.

Cooking Day

Setting aside a couple of hours one day a week to prepare meals will save you a lot of time in the long run. If you wish to eat healthy, home-cooked meals every day, some sort of preparation is a given. It will also save you money, especially if you prepare lunch boxes.

Use your cooking day to make something that you really enjoy, and that you can eat several times that week. Let us say that you really enjoy chicken and salmon, and cook about 2 pounds of each or more, depending on your needs. You can combine them with carbohydrate dishes, such as fake risotto with spelt, and red onion quinoa, which can both be eaten cold or warm. Perhaps you will even prepare a few sauces or salsas that you can store in the fridge if you don't end up using them up that same week. The next week, you can cook some more sauces on your cooking day, and soon enough you will have your own little store of delicious flavor additions to vary your food.

Make it a habit to cook for several meals while you are at it, even if it isn't your designated cooking day. If you live alone, you can cook a whole package of pasta or a fish stew that lasts over several meals. That way you won't have to cook as often, but you'll have leftovers to make snacks and lunch boxes.

Isn't it boring to live off of leftovers? No, it needn't be. The idea behind this book is to give you options on how to vary basic foods. Many were chosen because they are tasty whether you eat them cold or warm. A chicken fillet combined with freshly sautéed beans and guacamole will taste pretty different from a chicken fillet that you serve with stir-fried cauliflower with ginger, quinoa, and a green sauce with coriander and lime. You can also slice up the chicken fillet into a fake risotto with spelt, and flavor it with some black olives. There are endless delicious options. Other recipes in this book are for small meals that you can throw together in just a few minutes, and you can use them to com-plement or vary larger batches of basic dishes. Last but not least, the flavor options—sauces, salsas, and pesto—play a very important role in providing variety. A spoon of salsa or pesto can transform leftovers into an entirely new meal.

Food Economy

Economically speaking, you'll benefit from planning your grocery run ahead of time, and cooking large batches at once. Emergency solutions are usually expensive solutions. A protein shake may be an acceptable snack, but if you prepare something yourself, you cut the cost in half. Ready-to-eat, frozen meals are offered in many variations today. However, they tend to be a lot more expensive than if you cook them from scratch. The price tag might look enticing at first, but if you take into account how many ounces of quality produce, such as meat and vegetables, the frozen dinner contains, it all of a sudden seems like an expensive option. The majority of such meals consist of rice, potatoes, or sauce made with unhealthy fats, and starch, which also contributes to a high GI value.

It is pretty much a necessity to think economically if you want to eat healthy. There are plenty of very expensive health food options. Finding good-value alternatives can be quite the challenge. That's why this book emphasizes recipes that call for produce that is marked with good price tags most of the year.

Here are our best tips on how to save money:

Buy whole pieces. Learn how to fillet the salmon—or find a store where they do it for free. An entire salmon usually costs a lot less. Buy your meat in big pieces as well. A roast beef doesn't need to be sautéed whole, you can slice up the desired amount, and sauté only the portion you want to eat. Whole pieces of meat last longer than sliced meat, and you can store a piece like that for an entire week in the fridge, if it is fresh when you buy it. Large economy packs are useful too, as long as they contain something that you can make good use of.

Avoid semi-processed foods. Yes, it is convenient to buy hummus, tapenade, salsa, and tomato pesto. It is also very expensive. You can really save some money by making these meal additions from scratch, but use your common sense. Sometimes, it is worth spending the money to avoid the work in your kitchen.

Seize the opportunity—let the price tag decide. If you know what basic foods you are looking for, decide what additions you need once you are in the store. Make it a habit to pass the meat counter, the fish counter, and the vegetables to scan the price tags, and the quality of course, to decide what seems like a good choice that day. Allow that to be your guide in deciding what to cook, and feel free to bring home a little bit extra to store it in the freezer, and cook it up later in the week.

Use your freezer wisely. Most people have limited space in their freezer, so it is important to use it wisely. Protein sources such as fish, chicken, and meat take up a lot less space than vegetables. You are also more likely to save money if you buy these things in large packages. The protein source is usually the most expensive portion of your meal. Other smart choices to keep in the freezer are flavor additions, because a small amount can make a big difference. You can freeze grated ginger, fresh squeezed lemon, or chopped, fresh chili in ice cube trays, and transfer the ice cubes to a plastic box. Herbs such as parsley and dill are excellent to store in the freezer.

Meal boxes. The most important tip for any working professional is to bring meal boxes to work. A restaurant lunch usually costs over 10 dollars—and you can't control the nutritional value. Your homemade, healthy lunch rarely costs more than 3 dollars, even if it contains a nice piece of fish or meat. You can use the money you save with your lunch boxes to invest in high quality produce. It's a great improvement for many people. Not only are you saving money, but you are also eating better and healthier than before. The lunch box may just be the most helpful tip for achieving your fitness goals. Many of the recipes in this book include tips for your lunch boxes.

The Right Tools

Just like certain sports require certain equipment to achieve the best possible results, you will need the right tools to succeed in the kitchen. No one wants to run a marathon in the wrong type of shoes. Or exercise at a gym with broken fitness equipment. The same rule applies in the kitchen.

It's not about getting the latest technology when it comes to cooking equipment. What you need are basic, high-quality tools. Go through the list below, and mark the tools you need to buy. Cooking with good utensils is more fun and will save you time. Look at it as an investment in your health. A good knife or a cast-iron pan costs a little bit more, but is likely to last a lifetime if you care for it.

Digital scale. You probably want to track how much food you consume if you want to achieve the best possible results in your workout. However, the scale is also an excellent tool for your cooking needs. Instead of having to measure everything in cups and tablespoons, you can easily place your bowl on the scale, and add the ingredients directly. Some produce is difficult to measure without using a scale, such as parmesan, which can be packed very densely into a cup measure. The scale will help you get the correct amount. Produce such as fresh ginger is easy to

place on the scale, then peel it and grate it. Measuring grated ginger with a tablespoon can easily become a messy job, and it won't be as accurate. Produce such as onion and garlic vary in size. A measure, such as "one onion" or "one garlic clove," isn't very specific if the weight isn't provided.

Meat thermometer. We recommend that you get one. You'll turn your chicken, salmon, roast beef, and lamb steak into a success when you are able to read their inner temperature. A standard model meat thermometer only costs a few dollars, but even more advanced models are worth their price.

Timer/egg timer. One of the easiest ways to fail in the kitchen is to forget the food in the oven. Rid yourself of that risk by making it a habit to use a timer. You can also use it to track the cooking time on different produce.

Four knives. You will need a little peeling knife, which can be fairly inexpensive. Invest in a high-quality chef's knife. Most people also like to keep a serrated bread knife in their kitchen. A fillet knife is necessary if you want to fillet your fish.

At least two pots. One small, for cooking grains, such as bulgur and rice, or sauces, and one large pan for pasta, vegetables, and stews. It may be practical to have a thick-bottomed pan to fry onions or meat, and then add remaining ingredients, without having to use a frying pan and transfer the contents to a pan. A nice pot also looks lovely on the kitchen table.

At least one frying pan, preferably a large one with a lid. Cast iron pans are great because they release iron into the food that is taken up by our bodies. It is important to look after them properly, so that they don't get rusty.

Grater. A regular grater is fine, just make sure that it has both a fine and a coarse side.

Colander and a fine-mesh sieve. If you tend to cook a lot of vegetables, you may need to get two colanders. One to rinse the vegetables, and one to get rid of the cooking water. If you can stack them on top of each other they won't take up much space when you store them.

Bowls for mixing food. Three to four in various sizes, preferably of the same model, so that you can stack them and save storage space. Try to find bowls with lids—practical when you want to store food. It is a bonus if they are pretty, and you can place them on the serving table. The more functions, the better.

Wooden ladles. Sure, there are many different kitchen tools in metal, plastic, or expensive, high-tech materials such as silicone, which is resistant to extreme temperatures and easy to clean. However, wooden tools are cheap, they come in many different models, and they are excellent in the kitchen. You can even use wooden spatulas, and stock up on several since they are very affordable.

A spatula is invaluable when you want to transfer sticky dips and sauces to a different bowl. Definitely worth its price to avoid any mess.

A baking brush to cover food with olive oil, or any flavor addition. Silicone brushes are more expensive, but they are easier to clean and resistant to high heat.

Three cutting boards. Nothing is more irritating than running out of cutting boards, or having one that is too small when you are preparing a vegetable stir fry. Plastic cutting boards are inexpensive, practical, and they take up little storage space.

Mortar. Nothing can replace the mortar and pestle. Freshly ground spices have much more flavor than the ones you buy ground. You can also use the mortar for nuts and chili, which can be difficult to crush in any other way. Mortars are commonly made out of stone, but come in many other materials.

Pepper mill. Freshly ground black pepper, or white pepper, is an ingredient in almost every recipe in this book. Sometimes, salt and freshly ground pepper is all you need. Store-bought ground pepper doesn't compare to freshly ground pepper, because it has usually lost its aroma by the time you use it. A high-quality pepper mill might be the simplest way for you to turn each meal into a little party treat.

Potato peeler. Go with quality. Peeling carrots and beets can be painful with a dull peeler.

Mandoline. This is not a necessary tool, but if you get one, you'll never want to be without it again. Being able to quickly cut up vegetables into beautiful slices or sticks opens up the possibilities to enjoy healthy greens. It costs around 10 bucks or more. Always protect your fingers by using the holder for the vegetables.

Blender or hand mixer. Some recipes (i.e. hummus) require a blender or a hand mixer.

Plastic containers to store food in the fridge, freezer, and to cook things in the microwave. Use the same size you would use for your lunch boxes. They should be able to contain about 34 oz (1 liter), and are preferably low and wide. You'll also need a smaller size to store various flavorings, or for a portion of rice, bulgur, or quinoa. It may be practical to get a large container as well, about 68 oz (2 liters), to use for freezing vegetables.

Learning How to Cook

If you aren't used to cooking food, you may feel a bit reluctant to start. Many people think it is difficult, boring, and time consuming. Not true.

If you are feeling insecure in the kitchen, begin with the simplest recipes in the book. It is very difficult to mess up oven-roasted chicken fillets, roast beef, and salmon, especially if you have invested in a meat thermometer. Most sauces and salsas in the chapter about flavor additions are very easy to make. In the beginning, you'll do just fine with regular rice, pasta, and bulgur, which will allow you to focus on the vegetables. That's the part that most people neglect. The chapter on vegetables contains many simple recipes.

Once you have the basic routines down, it will be easier to tackle the more advanced recipes. But you shouldn't worry about it, because this book was intended for anyone who doesn't have much cooking experience or time to spend in the kitchen.

Despite that, you are bound to fail sometimes. When the chicken turns out too dry, or the sauce too salty, see it as a learning experience for the next time. The right attitude is just as important in cooking as in fitness. Don't give up, but try it again, and soon you'll have it down.

Eight Quick Tips to Improve Your Cooking Skills

The meal begins at the store. Invest in good produce, and spend a little bit of extra time to find them. Which store has the best vegetables, the freshest fish, and the best-value meat? Sometimes, it might be worth the extra mile to buy good quality food. The fish seller, the butcher, and the vegetable grocer usually have the best produce, and the price isn't necessarily higher than at the regular grocery store. High quality is always a good choice, because each bite of a succulent salmon fillet will end up in your tummy, as opposed to a dry and dull piece of fish that probably won't make it further than the trash bag. However, it is good to keep track of the price as well.

Think in four colors. You eat with your eyes as much as with your mouth. A bland and colorless plate won't stir your appetite. Colorful vegetables signify quality. If the tomatoes are deep red, and the savoy cabbage is dark green, they usually taste great too. Today, it is known that the color of the vegetable correlates with its content of minerals, vitamins, trace elements, and antioxidants. Eating colorful foods equals a varied and healthy diet.

Dare to ask. Great staff is always willing to give you advice about produce. Many items that may not be in stock can be ordered if you ask. If you eat something delicious at a friend's house, or a restaurant, ask them how they cooked it. Not knowing everything about food is nothing to be ashamed of, and if you never ask, you will never know.

You decide. Does grated apple taste delicious with pork tenderloin? Does the sauce need more salt? Is the salmon cooked—or terribly over-cooked? You decide. Forget about the rules, combine what you want, and use whatever spices tickle your senses. If you want to eat olives with everything, do so. The only way to become a good cook is to trust your intuition and taste buds.

Taste, smell, touch. Use all your senses when you buy food, and when you cook it. Sure, you shouldn't squeeze an avocado to the point of breaking it just to find out if it is ripe. But you can lift it in your hand to feel it. Practice will make you better at it. Smell fresh herbs, such as basil and coriander, before you buy them. If they don't have any aroma, chances are they are tasteless. If the fish doesn't look fresh—shiny, but firm and dry—don't buy it. If the meat doesn't smell good when you open the package, be cautious, and don't buy from the same provider next time. Also, make it a habit to taste the food, not only once it is done, but during the entire cooking process. Did you sauté the onion enough? If you don't sample it, you won't learn to recognize it for next time.

Dare to experiment. There is a saying that a good recipe works even if you change some of the steps. We have already provided you with different options on how to vary the recipes in this book, but don't stop at that. Let your imagination inspire you to create new variations. Eventually, you will be able to divert from the recipes entirely, and improvise your own meals. Be daring and try things that you might think you may not like. Perhaps you had a bad taste experience the first time you tried it because it wasn't properly prepared. We always say that there aren't any boring vegetables, but you need to know how to cook them.

Take your time. Time is valuable, and it may be difficult to find it for cooking. However, if you want to learn and enjoy the process, it requires a little bit of patience. Take the time to feel what you are in the mood for, and perhaps try something new. Allow enough time, so that in case you fail you can still make something else. That extra time is especially valuable when you are cooking for people other than yourself. Many of the dishes in this book are great on the buffet table, and can be combined into a real feast. If you are cooking up a buffet for your guests, don't worry too much about getting everything perfect. Taste is an individual matter, and each person will have their own preference.

Repeat. Have you ever tried a recipe, but not quite succeeded? Try it again. Analyze what went wrong, and try to fix it. It becomes a learning experience, rather than when you constantly move on to new recipes.

Nutrition in Practice

What you eat will impact your workout results. With all the current diet trends, alarm reports, and opinions by self-nominated experts at the gym, it is not easy to know what to believe. Naturally, it seems that one needs maximum nutrition knowledge to achieve the desired results. That's not the case. Here, we will teach you all you need to know.

The basis for a successful diet is very simple: variety, and high-quality produce. You risk nutritional deficiency if you always eat the same things. You can get all the necessary nutrients from regular foods. Sure, you may need to eat a little bit more of certain foods to cover your needs if you exercise a lot, but that's all. Allow yourself to enjoy delicious, home cooked meals, rather than reaching for the vitamin bottle. It's healthier, cheaper, and more environmentally friendly.

Protein to Repair and Build

Protein has many important functions. It repairs, builds, and maintains muscle mass, and many other types of body tissue, such as skin, hair, nails, tendons, ligaments, inner organs, and the skeleton.

Proteins can be found in hormones where they act as cell messengers, and are included in the cell membranes, where they control the transportation of nutrients and fluids that enter and exit the cells. Proteins affect the fluid balance in the blood and bodily tissues, and are the building blocks for antibodies—part of the immune system—and enzymes that are necessary for digestion and many other important bodily functions.

If you are exercising intensely, your body requires more protein. A person who doesn't work out only requires about 0.03 oz (0.8 grams) of protein per 2.2 pounds (1 kilogram) of body weight per day, but a person who is exercising on a regular basis needs about 0.04–0.07 oz (1.2–2 grams) of protein per 2.2 pounds (1 kilogram) of body weight a day. There are several reasons why:

People who exercise have greater muscle mass than people who don't, and exercising breaks down muscle mass. Therefore, there is more muscle mass to repair and maintain.

– Amino acids—components of protein that provide about 5 to 15 percent of the energy that is used up during exercise. The amount of protein that is used for energy increases when the body runs out of carbohydrates as an energy source. Contrary to what many people believe, endurance training uses up more protein than weight lifting and other sports that require a lot of physical strength.

– When you exercise, you tend to lose some of the protein through urination.

Despite the increased need for protein when exercising, most people get sufficient amounts through their diet, provided that they eat enough and stick to a balanced and varied diet. People who eat a varied diet automatically consume high biological value proteins, while vegetarians—who don't eat meat, fish, eggs, or dairy—have to be more cautious when planning their meals. Vegetable source proteins need to be combined to produce high biological value proteins, but it doesn't have to happen in the same meal, as long as they are combined during the same day.

Animal derived proteins come from meat, fish, poultry, eggs, and dairy. The most important vegetable derived proteins can be found in beans, lentils, chickpeas, nuts, seeds, and soybean products such as tofu. This book is divided into protein sources, carbohydrates sources, vegetables, and flavor additions so that you can easily combine your own meals for a varied and delicious diet. Just remember that several of the flavor additions and the vegetable dishes provide you with additional, valuable proteins. For examples, look at the hummus variations on pages 156–157, and the Spinach Salad with Almonds and Orange Dressing on page 106. The main courses also contain clues on how to increase the protein value in a meal. In the Baltic herring and feta gratin on page 66, the feta cheese provides the meal with extra protein, and the Chickpea Stew from North Africa on page 100 can be packed with as much protein as you desire, all while you get rid of leftovers.

Fats Provide Us with Important Energy

Physical exercise requires a lot of energy and fats give us the highest energy value per gram—9 calories per gram, compared to the energy value of proteins and carbohydrates, which provide us with 4 calories per gram. People who exercise require more energy, so it is important that they eat enough fat to not fall short of their energy need to prevent their performance and health from suffering. No matter how delicious a meal is, nobody wants to eat huge piles to consume enough energy value. Fats are also important in order for the body to be able to take up the fat-soluble vitamins A, D, E, and K. Fat shortage can lead to malnutrition. If you work out, fats also function as carbohydrate savers. When we exercise, the body uses a blend of carbohydrates and fats for fuel. However, our carbohydrate deposits are limited, while a thin and fit person's fat deposits last a lot longer than we are able to exercise. As long as the body has access to a sufficient amount of fat in its fuel storage, it will save the carbohydrates and you will have the energy to exercise longer. Exercising in general, but especially endurance training, tends to increase the body's ability to use fat as a source of energy.

In other words, you don't need to be afraid to include fats in your diet if you are exercising. Most workout enthusiasts try to avoid excessive fat at any price. Endurance training athletes want as "little fat as possible to carry around," and most people who exercise want to look defined, which requires a low percentage of body fat. The trick is to reach a point where you get enough fat to maximize performance, but without storing too much fat. That point lies in keeping your fat intake somewhere between 20 and 30 percent of your total energy intake. If you find it difficult to maintain a healthy weight and are constantly on the border of too little body fat, you should increase the fat value. However, if you easily gain weight, including fat weight, you should gear towards the lower value. Experiment to find what works best for you.

Different types of fat affect our health and shape differently. We should avoid certain kinds of fats, such as hydrogenated fats, partially hydrogenated fats, and trans fats. Those types of fats are often found in industrially processed foods, so the simplest way to cut them out of your diet is to cook your meals from scratch. It is important to balance the different fats in a meal. If the intake of saturated fats is high at the cost of polyunsaturated fats, it increases the risk of cardiovascular diseases, and may increase the risk of cancer and diabetes. A maximum of 10 percent of our daily calories should come from saturated fats. Remember, balance is important. Saturated fats are not dangerous, and there is no reason to eliminate them from your diet. Many people that are trying to lose weight tend to exclude meat and dairy from their diet out of fear of saturated fats. It is unnecessary to do so, and can make you miss out on a lot of important nutrients. For best results, let polyunsaturated and unsaturated fats make up the majority of your fat intake. Below are simple tips on how to get your fat intake in order:

- Continue to eat meat, but choose meat where you can cut away the fat strip after it is cooked, not before, because then the meat will turn out dry, dull, and lean.
- First and foremost, choose real meat, and decrease your intake of processed meat products such as sausage.

- Increase your fish consumption, including fish with a high fat content, such as salmon, mackerel, and Atlantic/Baltic herring. Eat fish at least 2–3 times a week. Studies show that an increased consumption of fish decreases the risk of cardiovascular diseases, most likely because of the healthy omega-3 fatty acids. Dishes such as Quick *gravlax* with lime and ginger on page 60, and Speedy Salmon with Coconut and Jalapeño on page 62, provide you with plenty of omega-3. Whenever possible, choose MSC (Marine Stewardship Council) certified fish. Vary between wild-caught and farm-raised fish. Wild-caught fish contains a higher value of omega-3, but is usually more expensive.

Use healthy oils when cooking, and use flavor additions that contain ingredients such as oils, nuts, seeds, olives, and avocado. Homemade Red Pesto on page 159, Rapeseed Oil with Fresh Turmeric on page 150, Tapenade on page 163, and Coconut Pesto with Green Chili on page 152, are good examples. They contain polyunsaturated and unsaturated fats. Then the meal will contain enough fat for you to feel full even if you eat a smaller serving of meat.

Carbohydrates—An Indispensable Source of Energy

Carbohydrates are our most important energy source. Compared with proteins and fats, which the body is able to store in large quantities, carbohydrates can only be stored in smaller amounts. You can easily use up your carbohydrates during a very hard or long workout session. We experience noticeable symptoms of a lack of carbohydrates even when we are just running low; we don't feel like we can do much more, or exercise as hard for a prolonged time. Without sufficient carbohydrates it will take us longer to recover between workout sessions. If you need more time to recuperate between exercise sessions, it is a sign that you shouldn't work out as much. If you feel like you don't have the strength to put much effort in, or can't exercise for very long, or as often as you'd like, this tends to lead to worsened workout results. A sufficient carbohydrate intake is necessary for you to have a successful workout. In addition, carbohydrates keep your cholesterol and fat levels in check, and contribute to healthy digestion by keeping your intestines in shape with their dietary fiber. Carbohydrates also contribute to your body's ability to absorb nutrients and water. They are also the brain's favorite fuel. A lack of carbohydrates leads to drowsiness, exhaustion, lack of focus, and makes you more susceptible to infections. Oversensitivity and irritation are typical signs that your brain hasn't gotten enough carbohydrate fuel.

The importance of carbohydrates for physical and mental health and your performance ability can't be stressed enough. Trend diets, such as LCHF and Atkins, unfortunately have spread a fear of carbohydrates, which has caused many people to exclude carbohydrates from their diet. However, if you are exercising several times a week, and skipping your carbohydrates, your workout results will worsen, and you can even become ill. Everything in moderation is always best.

GI for Better Fitness Results

Glycemic index, GI, measures how fast carbohydrates transform into blood sugar. Slow carbohydrates, GI < 60, take a long time to transform into blood sugar, medium-fast carbohydrates, GI 60–90, are turned into glucose at an intermediate speed, and fast carbohydrates, GI>90, raise blood sugar levels very quickly.

The body benefits from steady blood sugar levels. If the glucose levels drop too low, we feel tired, irritated, depressed, or restless, and we will have a hard time focusing on anything. The brain, which first and foremost uses blood sugar as fuel, sends signals to the body when it has an energy emergency, which usually manifests as a sweet tooth, or strong hunger. If your blood sugar levels are too high, they lead to destructive processes in the body over time, which can manifest in various forms, such as cardiovascular diseases, blindness, Alzheimer's disease, or dementia, as well as early aging. The body regulates high blood sugar levels by releasing insulin, a hormone that lowers glucose levels. Insulin ensures that the blood sugar is taken up by the muscles and liver, where it is transformed into glycogen, which is the storage form of carbohydrates. Insulin stimulates muscle building, but also fat storage in the fat cells.

When insulin is working at normal levels, it is released in moderate amounts to take care of the blood sugar levels in the body. That means you have good insulin sensitivity. If the receptors that read the blood sugar levels in the body are dysfunctional, the body will need to release more insulin in order for the muscles and liver to be able to absorb the insulin. That lowers the function of the receptors further, and eventually more insulin will need to be released in the body to handle the blood sugar. This easily leads to obesity. The muscle building effect of insulin deteriorates as the muscles lose their ability to absorb insulin as there are fewer receptors. People who work out regularly tend to have better insulin sensitivity than people who don't exercise, but diet will still come into play when it comes to the insulin levels released in the body. A diet that is high in saturated and hydrogenated fats lowers the insulin sensitivity. Likewise, you will experience the same effect if you eat a diet that mostly consists of fast carbohydrates. In addition, our insulin sensitivity worsens if we don't eat enough carbohydrates. A deficient insulin sensitivity contributes to more body fat, and muscle loss, or an inability to gain muscle mass. As a workout enthusiast, you will benefit from exercising and eating to maintain healthy insulin levels.

There are several trend diets that were created around the idea of glycemic index: the GI—diet and the Montignac diet are among the most popular. Other famous diets based on the same idea: the ISO—diet, and the South Beach diet, which call for a carbohydrate intake of mainly slow carbohydrates. That may be a smart strategy if you want to be healthy, but if you are exercising a lot your body requires certain conditions, depending on the type of exercise you perform and your workout goals. With the glycemic index in mind, you can customize your diet to help you achieve the desired results as fast as possible. We will explain what this means in practice a little bit further along in this book. The most important thing to remember is that if you are exercising a lot, your body requires more carbohydrates than what most trendy diets recommend.

Vitamins—Vital Nutrients

In order for certain chemical reactions to occur in the cells, vitamins are required. Certain vitamins are needed for the cells to convert carbohydrates, proteins, and fats into energy. Some vitamins work in teams with minerals; vitamin C facilitates the body's ability to absorb iron, and vitamin D helps the body to take up calcium and phosphorus. If we don't get enough vitamins we become ill, and when you exercise your body requires more vitamins. This need can be covered in your diet, and few people need dietary supplements. Taking supplements in the form of individual vitamins can even have a negative effect on your health and performance ability. To ensure adequate vitamin intake, make sure to consume enough energy and to eat a varied diet with a lot of vegetables, root vegetables, fruit, and berries, as they are packed with vitamins. Try steaming or microwaving vegetables and root vegetables, because a short cooking time will retain their vitamins. The microwave is seldom used as a cooking device, but it is one of your greatest assets in the kitchen, provided that you keep track of the cooking time and don't overcook the food. In the recipe section, Niclas explains how you can cook several dishes in the microwave. Some examples include dishes that are packed with vitamins and antioxidants: Pink Coleslaw (page 102), Speedy Salmon with Coconut and Jalapeño (page 62), Black Pepper Beans cooked in the microwave (page 120), and Quick steamed plaice in the microwave (page 72).

Our Mineral Intake Should Come From Our Diet

Minerals should come from our diet. They strengthen and structure our skeleton, and affect the fluid balance in our blood and bodily tissues. They function as bridges for electrical impulses, they participate in muscle contractions, nerve reactions, and many other processes in the body. A varied diet that fulfills the body's energy requirement is usually enough for people that work out to get the minerals they need. People who exercise a lot on an intense level may benefit from making sure to get enough calcium and iron. Dairy products, dark green leafy greens, legumes, and soymilk contain a lot of calcium. A small serving of spinach can provide you with 30–40 percent of the recommended daily intake of iron, which makes Spinach salad with almonds and orange dressing on page 108 the perfect calcium boost, because it also contains cooking yogurt. Some produce, such as orange juice, often contains added calcium. Meat, poultry, fish, and seafood contain a lot of iron. Calcium levels are also fairly high in legumes, dark-green leafy greens, and dried fruit. Cooking food in a cast iron skillet increases the iron levels in the food.

Antioxidants: Our Shield Against Free Radicals

Antioxidants are chemical compounds that inhibit oxidation in living organisms. Oxidation occurs naturally as a result of cellular respiration, during which free radicals increase in the body. Severe oxidation increases the risk for cardiovascular diseases, cancer, and other illnesses. In addition, oxidative stress speeds up the aging process. Physical exercise increases free radicals in the body; the harder the exercise, the more oxidative stress. The body builds its own defense system against free radicals automatically when you exercise on a regular basis. Antioxidants in food further protect us against free radicals. Vitamin C, vitamin E, and beta-carotene are considered antioxidants. Glutathione, alpha lipoic acid, and carotenoids such as lycopene, which can be found in tomatoes, are other examples. Other antioxidants include flavonoids, which can be found in red wine, tea, coffee, chocolate, cinnamon, olive oil, and other substances. The best way to increase your antioxidant intake is to eat a lot of fruit, berries, vegetables, and root vegetables, and include foods that are rich in flavonoids into your diet. Switch it up, and choose colorful variations. A strong color is usually a sign that the produce contains a lot of antioxidants. The vegetable dishes in this book are guaranteed to contain a lot of antioxidants and vitamins, and the flavor additions will also give you a good nutrition boost. Pomegranate salsa with walnuts on page 154 is a great example. So is the Ill-green sauce on page 144.

About the Nutritional Values in the Recipes

We have included the nutritional value for all the recipes in this book, except for the flavor additions. You can find tables with their nutritional value at www.matforresultat.se. We always begin with the energy and nutritional value for the entire batch. We imagine that you cook the entire batch each time, and then divide the food into serving sizes. Each recipe also provides you with the number of servings per batch, and the nutritional details for each portion.

We imagine that you eat five meals a day: breakfast, morning snack, lunch, afternoon snack, and dinner. Below is an estimation of how your total energy intake is distributed during the course of the day:

Breakfast: 25% of the total energy intake
Morning Snack: 12.5% of the total energy intake
Lunch: 25% of the total energy intake
Afternoon Snack: 12.5% of the total energy intake
Dinner: 25% of the total energy intake

This book provides you with recipes for meals that are good both for lunch and dinner, and the serving sizes are estimated to provide about 25 percent of your daily energy intake. If you prefer to consume less of your energy intake during lunch or dinner, and rather eat more during one of your snack meals, adjust the serving sizes accordingly. The portions are estimated to fulfill four different energy needs:

- If you are in heavy/intense strength/weight lifting training several times a week, and your goal is to increase your muscle mass.
- If you perform endurance training, such as running, cycling, cross-country skiing, or similar sports a few times a week. Or if you are in long distance training, such as speed training, or interval training, and your goal is to increase both endurance and speed.
- When your goal is to get more defined, through heavy/intense weight lifting, combined with intense burning workouts so that you maintain your muscle mass, while decreasing your body fat.
- If your goal is to lose weight, we imagine that you are over-weight, and recently began an exercise regimen that combines weight lifting and cardio training, perhaps 2–3 times a week, but are still at a beginner level.

When we calculated the energy value required for weight lifting, and definition training, we imagined a man in his 30s. For the energy value behind the endurance training, and the weight loss program, we had a 30-something woman in mind. In both cases, we imagined that they are regular people with jobs that don't require a lot of physical movement.

These are clues to help you adjust the serving sizes so that they fulfill your individual needs. There are several factors that play into how much energy you need to consume each day:

- How much you work out: how many times a week, and how long each session is.
- How active you are in your everyday life, whether you walk or bike to and from work, or how often you take the stairs instead of the elevator.
- Whether you are physically active at your job, or not.
- Your workout of choice.
- The intensity of your workout.
- Your total body weight, and your muscle mass: the more muscles, the more active body mass that needs to be provided with energy 24 hours a day. In general, men have more muscle mass and less body fat than women, which means that men require a higher energy intake than women.
- Genetics.
- Younger people that are still developing require more energy than adults who are fully developed.

There are many factors that matter when it comes to adjusting the serving sizes according to your exact needs. Listen to your body: Do you feel full? How do you feel during your workout? Analyze your results after a month, and fine-tune the adjustments accordingly. How much energy you need will also change during the year, depending on if you are following an easier or harder exercise regimen, so it is important to use your common sense. Use your judgment to tune in to your needs. Don't let dieticians that claim one particular diet is the only answer make the decision for you. Everybody is different. One type of diet couldn't possibly be right for everyone. We all come from different backgrounds, lifestyles, preferences, and we all set different goals for ourselves. Figure out what works for you, and stick to it.

Our starting point is that if you are exercising intensely, you require about 1.2 to 2 grams of protein per 2.2 pounds (1 kg) of body weight a day, and your fat intake should be somewhere between 20 and 30 percent of your daily energy intake. In other words, 20–30 percent of your total calorie intake per day should come from fat. If you are going for 2600 calories per day, 520–780 calories should derive from fat, or about 58–87 grams of fat per day. We imagine that if you are in endurance training, you'll need a higher carbohydrate intake than if you aren't working out as intensely, but are striving to lose weight. Because each recipe is divided into proteins, carbohydrates, vegetables, and flavor additions, it is easy to adjust the servings sizes between the various sections if you wish to stick to a certain trend diet. You may discover that you have more energy, and are able to work out a lot harder if you divide the servings differently than we have suggested in this book. Naturally, you should take that into account and plan your diet accordingly. Remember: There is no exact diet or nutritional make up that is best for all. You know best what works for you by trying different ways.

Carbohydrates, a Comparison

Below, you can compare energy content, GI, and other nutritional values in some common carbohydrate sources. The normal serving size is intended for a person who doesn't have a very active lifestyle, and who is trying to lose weight. The workout portion is for someone who is moderately active. Someone who works out a lot, or who has a very effective digestive system, may need larger servings. The "2/5 cup weighs" measures the food when it is uncooked. The GI values are for cooked food. Notice that the GI is lower if you allow the food to cool after you have cooked it. A good rule of thumb for a normal serving size is to imagine that you should be able to fit your cooked pasta or potatoes in the palm of your hand.

Produce	Calories/ 100 g	Protein (g)/ 100 g	Fat (g) / 100 g	Carbs(g)/ 100 g	Fiber (g)	GI	2/5 cup weighs (g)	1 normal serving (g)	1 work out serving (g)
Bulgur	324	12	1	65	11	48	80	40–60	80–100
Couscous	350	13	0.5	72	5	65	80	40–60	80–100
Spelt, whole	326	13.5	3	60	8	68	100	80	100–120
Pasta, i.e. penne	350	12	1.5	72	2.5	appr 60		85–100*	175*
Whole grain pasta	330	13	2.5	62	9	appr 55		85–100*	175*
Potatoes	76	1.8	0.1	16	1.5	80-135**	1st = 85–100	175 g	250–350g
Quinoa	370	13	4.5	69	11	35	80	40–60	80–100
Rice, basmati	353	7	2.5	74	3	83	100	50–75	100–125
Rice, parboiled	350	7.5	1	76	1.6	68	100	50–75	100–125
Rice, whole grain	353	7.5	2	73	3	79	100	50–75	100–125
Brown rice	354	7	2.5	74	3	80	100	50–75	100–125
Wild rice	360	8	2	76	5	57	100	50–75	100–125
Arborio rice	360	6.5	0.5	79	1	69	100	50–75	100–125

* Regular pasta, and wheat pasta dry in box, not fresh pasta containing egg.
Observe that the GI value may vary depending on the contents of the pasta.
** = 80–90 for boiled potatoes, 117–135 for baked potatoes, 98–118 for mashed potatoes

Proteins

Oven Baked Chicken Breast Fillets

I usually buy chicken breast fillets in large packages to reduce the price per pound, and cook the entire package right away (six to seven fillets). It is an excellent way to prepare for the week's lunch boxes, for a quick snack, or a dinner later in the week. A baked fillet will last for an entire week if you store it in a sealed container in the fridge, otherwise you can freeze it. Oven baked fillets remain juicy even when you reheat them. You have the option of baking one, or all of them at the same time.

2.2 lbs (1 kg) chicken breast fillets
1 tbsp olive oil
1 tbsp butter

Heat up a skillet, preferably cast iron. Add the cooking fats and allow the butter to get a nice color. Sauté the fillets at a high heat for a minute or two on each side. Lift them with a spatula to brown the sides as well.

Transfer the fillets to an ovenproof dish and bake in the oven at 250 degrees for about 25 minutes. If the skillet is ovenproof, you can place the entire skillet with the fillets in the oven. It is recommended to use a meat thermometer that you stick into the thickest part of the fillet. Appropriate interior temperature should be about 155 degrees.

TIP: Before transferring the fillets to the oven, try rolling them in your favorite seasoning, or sprinkle some seasoning on top. Curry, Sichuan pepper, lemon zest, cumin, chili powder, garlic powder, black pepper, grated nutmeg, chopped nuts, or a blend are all excellent options.

CAMILLA'S COMMENT: Chicken fillets are delicious and provide a lean source of protein that can easily be flavored and combined in various ways—as a main course or a snack. They are smart and practical, and naturally you can replace them with turkey fillets, which are also sold in large economy packs.

	○	◍	●	●	●
Portion of Batch	$\frac{1}{1}$	$\frac{1}{5}$	$\frac{1}{5}$	$\frac{1}{5}$	$\frac{1}{8}$
Calories	1579	316	316	316	198
Protein (g)	275	55	55	55	34
Fat (g)	52	10	10	10	6.5
Carbohydrates (g)	0	0	0	0	0
Fiber (g)	0	0	0	0	0

Boiled Chicken Breast Fillets

This recipe is for 2.2 pounds (1 kg) of fillets, but you can also prepare it with less chicken. Boiled fillets can be stored in their own bouillon, and you can eat them cold with some rice and vegetables. You can heat them in the microwave, quickly fry them in a skillet, or slice them up and throw them into the wok with some vegetables. Another option is to slice up the cold chicken and toss the pieces into a filling salad, i.e. a Fake Risotto with Spelt (page 138), or together with some veggies and Tart Black Quinoa (page 142). Also check out my recipe for Hash with Chickpeas & Chicken on page 42.

2.2 lbs (1 kg) chicken breast fillets
1 ⅓–1 ¾ cups (3-4 dl) chicken bouillon
2 bay leaves
optional ⅕ cup (½ dl) Rapeseed Oil with Fresh Turmeric, see page 150
   (can be replaced with 1 teaspoon dried turmeric)

Place the fillets close together on the bottom of a pan. Pour enough bouillon into the pan to cover the fillets. Season with bay leaves and turmeric. Turn on the heat, and begin tracking cooking time once the bouillon starts to boil. Remove the pan from the heat after 10 minutes, and allow the fillets to sit in the hot bouillon for a few minutes. Make sure that the fillets are cooked by lifting one of them out of the pan and cutting it in half. The meat shouldn't be pink or raw, and the juices should run clear. If the meat or juices are pink, you need to cook the fillets a little bit longer.

TIP: Sometimes I cut up an onion and a few carrots, and add them to the pan with the chicken. The vegetables add a little bit of flavor to the chicken, and they are also a delicious addition on the plate. You can serve a sliced fillet with bouillon and vegetables as a soup, with a slice of hearty bread on the side.

CAMILLA'S COMMENT: Perfect basic food to keep in the fridge that you can combine with many sides to create various meals. Because chicken is such a lean source of protein, you can choose calorie-rich sides to pair it with.

	●	●	●	●	●
Portion of Batch	⅟₁	¼	¼	⅕	⅛
Calories	1474	368	294	294	184
Protein (g)	232	58	46	46	29
Fat (g)	58	14.5	12	12	7
Carbohydrates (g)	4	1	1	1	0.5
Fiber (g)	0	0	0	0	0

With Hearty Wheat Berry Salad (p. 136), and Pomegranate & Walnut Salsa (p. 154).

Grilled Chicken Thigh Fillets with Spicy Tamarind Paste

Chicken thighs are less expensive and less lean than chicken breast. That makes them an excellent choice to grill in the oven, because they won't easily turn dry. If you have made Super Spicy Tamarind Paste (page 158) and have some leftovers in the fridge, you can quickly mix up a little batch directly in the bowl with the chicken fillets. Divide the amount in the recipe by 4, and you'll have the perfect amount.

1 tbsp rapeseed oil
2.2 lbs (1 kg) chicken thigh fillets
1 ½–2 tablespoons Super Spicy Tamarind Paste

Set the oven on the grill setting, and heat to 425 degrees. Brush a baking tray with the oil. Cut the chicken fillets in half if they are very big. Place them in a plastic bowl with the tamarind paste and turn the fillets over so that they are covered in the spicy paste. Place them on the baking tray and grill for 10 minutes in the center of the oven, turn the pieces over, and grill for another 10 minutes.

CAMILLA'S COMMENT: Since this dish is so flavorful already, I recommend serving it with a simple carbohydrate choice, and some fresh vegetables. The portion sizes for those who are in endurance training or are trying to gain definition are large, so adjust the serving size accordingly.

Portion of Batch	⅓	¼	¼	¼	⅙
Calories	1284	321	321	321	214
Protein (g)	196	49	49	49	33
Fat (g)	54	13.5	13.5	13.5	9
Carbohydrates (g)	2	0.5	0.5	0.5	0
Fiber (g)	0	0	0	0	0

With Grilled White Cabbage (p. 92) and Spice Risotto (p. 132)

Hash with Chickpeas & Chicken

I tend to make this dish whenever I have leftover chickpeas and chicken in the fridge. Dried chickpeas that you soak yourself and cook (according to the instructions on the packaging) are delicious and economical. They will turn out extra yummy if you cook them in chicken bouillon. The cooked chickpeas will last at least a week if you store them in the fridge. However, you always have the option to buy canned chickpeas that are already cooked, and you can make this dish with a raw chicken fillet if you don't happen to have one that's already cooked.

14 oz (400 g) chickpeas, boiled
1 tbsp olive oil
1 tbsp butter
1 tsp sugar
1 small onion, red or yellow,
    chopped

1 chicken fillet about 5.6 oz (160 g),
cooked or raw
herb salt
black pepper

Heat up a skillet to medium or high heat. Sauté the chickpeas in oil and butter. Sprinkle with sugar—it will lift the flavor of the chickpeas and give them a crispy surface. Watch the chickpeas when you sauté them because they tend to pop away, similar to when you are popping popcorn. After about 2 minutes, they should have a nice color. Lower the heat, and add the onion. Sauté for about 2 more minutes before you add the chicken fillet. If you are using a cooked fillet, cut it into fairly big pieces. If you are using raw chicken, halve it lengthwise, before you slice it thinly. Sauté with the remaining ingredients for about 2 minutes, or until the chicken is cooked.

CAMILLA'S COMMENT: This is a great combo that is packed with protein, and a fair amount of carbohydrates. If you add more chickpeas, you'll have a complete main course that you can complete with some vegetables. The portion sizes for those who are in endurance training or are trying to gain definition are fairly large, so adjust the serving size accordingly.

GI · SYMBOL
60

Portion of Batch	1/1	1/3	1/3	1/3	1/5
Calories	968	323	323	323	194
Protein (g)	68	23	23	23	14
Fat (g)	146	49	49	49	29
Carbohydrates (g)	73	24	24	24	15
Fiber (g)	26	9	9	9	5

Black Pepper Coated Chicken Liver with Pecorino

You can usually find frozen chicken liver at a regular grocery store, but I tend to get mine at a local butcher, where the quality is better and the price lower. I then divide the fresh chicken liver into serving sizes that meet my needs and freeze them. These individual portions are excellent to pull out of the freezer when you run out of ideas.

17.5 oz (500 g) chicken liver
⅕ cup (25 g) graham flour
optional: 3 tbsp breadcrumbs
1 tsp salt
1 tsp freshly ground black pepper

1 tbsp olive oil
1 tbsp butter
⅖ cup (40 g) freshly grated pecorino, or parmesan
2 tbsp honey (liquid)

Chicken liver consists of two halves that are attached by a thin string. Cut the halves apart, and place them in a colander to drain them. Mix flour, breadcrumbs, salt, and pepper in a plastic bag, or in a plastic container with a lid. Place the liver in the bag or container, and seal. Shake thoroughly, until the liver is covered in the flour mix. Heat a skillet to medium heat, and add oil or butter. Sauté the liver for 3–4 minutes, and turn the pieces so that they get a nice color on all sides. Lower the heat, and cook for another 4–5 minutes. Chicken liver should be thoroughly cooked before you eat it, just like with any chicken meat. Feel free to cut one of the liver pieces in half to make sure that it looks even in color and that it is not raw in the middle. If it isn't ready, cook it for a little while longer. Sprinkle the liver with pecorino or parmesan, and drizzle with a little bit of honey before you serve it.

CAMILLA'S COMMENT: Liver is an excellent and inexpensive protein source that is packed with iron. Chicken liver has a milder flavor than any other type of liver, which is why it is popular even with people who usually don't like the taste of liver.

Portion of Batch	⅟₁	¼	⅕	⅕	⅙
Calories	1422	356	284	284	237
Protein (g)	125	31	25	25	21
Fat (g)	64	16	13	13	11
Carbohydrates (g)	81	20	16	16	13.5
Fiber (g)	9	2	2	2	1.5

With Red Bulgur (p. 135) and a little bit of sautéed spinach.

Sautéed Chicken Liver with Apple and Onion

The flavor of chicken liver is excellent with the crisp flavor of sautéed apples, combined with a sweet touch of balsamic vinegar.

1 yellow onion
17.5 oz (500 g) chicken liver
1 firm, red apple
1 tbsp olive oil
1 tbsp butter
1 tbsp balsamic vinegar
1 tbsp soy sauce
½ tsp salt
freshly ground black pepper
optional: a pinch of Sichuan pepper

Peel the onion, cut it in half, and cut into slices that are about 0.1–0.15 inches thick. Cut the pairs of chicken livers apart. Cut the apple into four pieces, remove the core, and cut cross-wise into slices that are about 0.1–0.15 inches thick. Sauté the onion in the oil and butter for a few minutes over medium heat. Turn up the heat as high as it goes, and add the chicken liver. Sauté for another 3 minutes, and turn the liver continuously. Add the apple slices, and sauté for a few minutes. Add vinegar, soy sauce, salt, and pepper. Lower the heat and cook over low heat for 4–5 minutes, preferably under a lid. If you've made the Szechuan Soy Sauce (page 146), you can use 2 tablespoons of it instead of the Sichuan pepper, soy sauce, and vinegar.

CAMILLA'S COMMENT: Apples are rich in fiber and full of oxidants, such as quercetin and catechin.

GI · SYMBOL
30

	●	●	●	●	●
Portion of Batch	⅟₁	⅓	⅓	⅓	¼
Calories	937	312	312	312	234
Protein (g)	100	33	33	33	25
Fat (g)	47	16	16	16	12
Carbohydrates (g)	28	9	9	9	7
Fiber (g)	2.5	1	1	1	0.5

Octopus Wok with Ginger & Garlic

I almost always keep a little bag of octopus in the freezer. It is an excellent and inexpensive source of protein, and you can easily thaw the amount needed in the microwave. Fresh coriander, parsley, chives, and other herbs are excellent to cut over the wok when you serve it.

17.5 oz (500 g) octopus, whole, or
    cut into circles
a large piece of ginger, peeled and
    grated (about 2.5 oz/70 g)
5 garlic cloves, pressed (about 0.5
    oz/15 g)
1 tsp salt
1 tsp sugar
1 tsp freshly ground black pepper

½ tsp cumin
1 lime, squeezed
2 red bell peppers
1 zucchini
10.5 oz (300 g) white cabbage,
    shredded
corn oil
1 tbsp fish sauce

Thaw the octopus and drain it in a colander. The easiest thing is to buy octopus that is already cut into rings or pieces. If you buy the octopus whole, begin by severing the head from the body. Rinse the head, and squeeze out the little "beak" and throw it out (see picture). Rinse the head if it has octopus innards on it. Rinse the tube-shaped body, and remove the cartilage (see photo). Cut into rings. You can cut the head in half, or sauté it whole, depending on how large it is.

- Peel the ginger, and grate it finely over a bowl so that you catch all the ginger juice. Press the garlic into the bowl, and add salt, sugar, black pepper, cumin, and half of the lime juice. Marinate the octopus in the mix for at least 30 minutes, but preferably for a few hours.
- Cut the vegetables into bite-sized pieces (read more about how to cook vegetables in a wok on page 80). Use different kinds of vegetables. You will need about 28 oz (800 g) cleaned and cut vegetables.
- Heat a skillet with corn oil at a high heat. Sauté the vegetables in 2–3 batches, turning them continuously so that they get a nice color on all sides. Transfer the vegetables to a pot or pan, and keep them warm under a lid. You'll need to fill the skillet with more oil in between the batches.
- Lift the octopus out of the marinade. Sauté it at high heat until it has a nice color. Once everything is sautéed, mix the vegetables with the octopus in the pot or pan. Transfer the pan to the heated stove, and cook at highest heat for a minute or two. Pour the marinade into the pot, together with the remaining lime juice and the fish sauce. Cover with a lid and turn the heat down. Allow to stand for a minute or two, depending on how crisp you want the vegetables. Serve with rice or quinoa.

CAMILLA'S COMMENT: Octopus is a great food, however, I've always felt insecure when it comes to cooking it. Now, I know what to do with it and this recipe is absolutely delicious. With this dish, you'll also get a good vegetable boost. All you need to do is add some carbohydrates, although there is never anything wrong with eating extra vegetables.

Portion of Batch	1/1	1/2	1/2	1/2	1/4
Calories	950	475	475	475	238
Protein (g)	98	49	49	49	25
Fat (g)	26	13	13	13	7
Carbohydrates (g)	80	40	40	40	20
Fiber (g)	20	10	10	10	5

GI • SLOW 30 TO 80

Octopus with Black Bean Sauce

This is a very versatile recipe, as you can replace the octopus with chicken, pork tenderloin, chicken liver, or salmon. You can also vary the vegetables according to what you happen to have in the fridge. You can find black bean sauce in Asian food markets. The jar will last for a few months after you open it if you keep it in the fridge.

17.5 oz (500 g) octopus, cut into pieces or rings
1 leek (about 12.5 oz/350 g)
2 large carrots (about 12.5 oz/350 g)
3 tbsp rapeseed oil
⅕ cup (about 50 ml) black bean sauce
1 tbsp fish sauce
1 tbsp soy sauce

Trim and clean the thawed octopus, and cut it into pieces, or rings if needed (see page 48–49). You can also use ready-made octopus rings (not breaded). Slice the leek and carrots into 0.15-inch-thick pieces.

First, sauté the carrots in a tablespoon of oil at very high heat for 2–3 minutes. Then add another tablespoon of oil, and sauté the leek together with the carrots for about the same amount of time. Transfer the sautéed vegetables to a pot or pan with a lid. Add another tablespoon of oil and sauté the octopus at high heat. Combine the octopus with the vegetables, and add the black bean sauce, the fish sauce, and the soy sauce. Cover with a lid, and heat over medium heat for a few minutes. Serve with white rice and one of the soy sauces on page 146–147.

CAMILLA'S COMMENT: You can combine the lean octopus with one of the more energy-rich carbohydrate options, and a vegetable serving.

			●	●	●
Portion of Batch	½₁	⅓	¼	¼	⅕
Calories	1110	370	278	278	222
Protein (g)	92	31	23	23	18
Fat (g)	52	17	13	13	10
Carbohydrates (g)	58	19	15	15	12
Fiber (g)	17	6	4	4	3

Quick Black Shellfish Risotto

You can use a store-bought fish and shellfish blend for this risotto that is inspired by the flavors of Thailand. You also have the option to mix your own blend with fish, mussels, octopus, crabsticks, and shrimp.

⅘ cup (130 g) wild rice
½ stalk lemon grass
½ tsp salt
optional: fresh red chili, preferably the piri piri kind
1 lime, freshly squeezed
2 tbsp fish sauce

1 tbsp ginger (about 15 g), grated
10.5 oz (300 g) fish fillets, octopus, and shellfish
1 tbsp neutral oil, i.e. corn oil
⅖ cup fresh coriander, chopped (about 20 g)

Rinse the rice or the quinoa thoroughly, and strain in a colander. Cook according to the directions on the packaging, but also add the lemongrass stalk (cut into large pieces), and ½ teaspoon of salt. It takes about half an hour to cook wild rice, which is a type of raw rice. The cooking time for black quinoa is about 20 minutes. Check on the rice, or the quinoa, regularly, and remove from the heat when it is almost cooked. Remove the lemongrass. Slice the chili and add it. Add most of the lime juice, the fish sauce, the ginger, and stir. Taste and add more fish sauce or lime juice, if needed. Sauté the fish rapidly in a hot skillet with the oil. Separate the octopus, fish/shrimp, and mussels. Sauté the octopus over high heat until it has a nice color. Set it aside. Sauté the fish and the shrimp at a medium temperature for a few minutes. Lower the heat, and add the mussels at the end—they should just barely get warm. Add the octopus back into the skillet, add the rice mix, and at last—the coriander.

If you are using a ready-to-use fish and shellfish blend, you can sauté everything together for a few minutes, before you add the rice mix, or you can separate the octopus and the mussels in the blend and cook it as above.

CAMILLA'S COMMENT: Raw wild rice is rich in antioxidants, and has a low GI value. In addition, it contains a lot of fiber. The servings sizes have been determined imagining that you will add a large vegetable serving with the rice.

GI · SYMBOL **46**

Portion of Batch	⅟₁	½	½	½	⅓
Calories	1073	537	537	537	358
Protein (g)	73	37	37	37	24
Fat (g)	16	8	8	8	5
Carbohydrates (g)	160	80	80	80	53
Fiber (g)	7	3.5	3.5	3.5	2

Fish Stew from Lamu

Along the east coast of Kenya and Tanzania—the Swahili coast—coconut, cinnamon, and cardamom are popular spices when cooking fish and shellfish. This simple recipe has a mild, exotic flavor. You can vary this dish by using different kinds of fish, but it also tastes excellent with one type of fish. A blend of various kinds will turn it into a party meal. I tend to use a frozen fish and shellfish blend, and add a jar of mussels and/or a little bit of octopus.

21–25 oz (600–700 g) fish, shrimp, octopus, mussels
1 tbsp cumin
cinnamon stick, about 1.2–1.6 inches long
1 tsp cardamom seeds
nutmeg, about 1/5 of a whole nutmeg
1 tsp freshly ground black pepper
1 tsp salt
6 allspice peppercorns

1 tsp chili powder
1 onion, sliced or chopped
2 garlic cloves, freshly pressed
2 tbsp rapeseed oil
4/5 cup (200 ml) coconut milk, 17% fat
1 jar tomatoes 14 oz (400 g), preferably cocktail tomatoes
1 tbsp fish sauce

First, sauté the spices with the onion and garlic in oil. The onion should turn soft and transparent at low heat, which takes about 5 minutes. Add coconut milk, tomatoes, and fish sauce. Simmer for about 10 more minutes. Fish, shrimp, octopus, and mussels should be thawed before you add them to the pot. Simmer carefully for 5 more minutes.

Serve with coconut rice or spiced rice. The African tomato salad on page 110 is from the same region in Africa, and will go nicely with this dish.

TIP: Make a double batch of the sauce and freeze it, preferably in smaller containers, so that you have a good serving size to take out when you want to heat some fish in it.

CAMILLA'S COMMENT: This dish is like a health boost, containing healthy fats, and packed with protein and heating spices (see page 180). Together with the sides recommended by Niclas, you get more of the same nutrients, and plenty of vitamins and antioxidants.

	●	●	●	●	●
Portion of Batch	1/1	1/4	1/4	1/4	1/6
Calories	1261	315	315	315	210
Protein (g)	121	30	30	30	20
Fat (g)	75	19	19	19	12.5
Carbohydrates (g)	22	5.5	5.5	5.5	4
Fiber (g)	11	3	3	3	2

GI · SYMBOL
15

Baked Salmon

The salmon pretty much bakes itself in the oven, which frees you up to prepare the rest of the meal. You can easily adjust the serving sizes to your needs, and you can cut up portions in the beginning, when the salmon is cold and can be easily weighed. You may want to cook a little bit extra to have some for your lunch boxes. You can keep a piece of the baked salmon in the fridge for several days, and you can reheat it in the microwave.

2.2 lbs (1 kg) salmon fillet with skin
salt
olive oil
optional: spices

Preheat the oven to 300 degrees. Rub the fish with salt, and brush with some olive oil. If you wish to add some spices, now is the time to sprinkle some over the salmon. You can also mix it into the olive oil before you brush it on. Garlic, curry, saffron, lemon pepper, cayenne pepper, lemon zest, and cumin are excellent spices to choose from.

I recommend using an oven thermometer to ensure that the salmon bakes perfectly. Stick it into the thickest part of the fish. Once the temperature reaches 118.4 degrees, it is done.

CAMILLA'S COMMENT: I find salmon to be one of the most delicious things one could eat. It's a good thing for me that it is so healthy. It is packed with protein and healthy fats. Leftovers are excellent to use in a filling salad, a delicious sandwich, or make a lovely snack by combining it with a small serving of one of the carbohydrate options.

Portion of Batch	⅟₁	¼	⅕	¼	⅙
Calories	1309	327	261	327	218
Protein (g)	206	51	41	51	34
Fat (g)	53	13	11	13	8
Carbohydrates (g)	0	0	0	0	0
Fiber (g)	0	0	0	0	0

Poached Cold Salmon

Poached cold salmon can be eaten as soon as it has cooled off a little bit, but it tastes best when cold. Whenever I cook 2 pounds or more, I tend to eat a piece that very same evening, and store the rest in the fridge. Then I can pull a fillet out of the fridge whenever, and serve a complete meal by adding vegetables and carbohydrates.

2.2 lbs (1 kg) salmon fillet
3²/₅ cups water (800 ml)
⅕ cup vinegar (50 ml), or alcoholic
    vinegar 12%
1 tbsp salt
5 white peppercorns
5 allspice peppercorns
2 bay leaves
1 yellow onion, cut into slices
1 carrot, cut into large pieces
optional: 1 small piece of celeriac, or
    a few stalks of celery
optional: 2–3 sprigs of dill

Remove the skin from the salmon fillet, using a fillet knife if you have one. Cut the salmon into portions that fit your nutritional needs, or cut into large squares (about 1.2 x 1.2 inches). Boil the water with the vinegar, spices, vegetables, and dill. Allow to boil for 5–10 minutes. Add the salmon pieces and boil for 1–2 minutes. Remove from the heat, and allow the salmon to cool in the water for 15–20 minutes. The remaining heat in the water will finish cooking the salmon. Immediately store the salmon you won't eat that day in the cooking liquid in the fridge.

TIP: If you aren't going to eat the vegetables in the liquid, you don't need to peel them as long as you rinse them. However, you may as well boil the vegetables that you want to eat in the liquid. Begin with a carrot and an onion (cut into pieces), then add fennel, cauliflower, beets, or zucchini. Remove them from the cooking liquid and set aside, before you poach the salmon. You can eat them lukewarm with the salmon, or reheat them in the microwave. Tapenade (page 163) or the tart Ill-green sauce (page 144) complement this dish nicely.

CAMILLA'S COMMENT: Salmon is an excellent source of protein, and provides you with healthy omega-3 fatty acids. Remember, the vegetables give this dish its GI value. If you aren't going to eat them, but use them solely to flavor the salmon, the GI value will be around 0 for this dish.

GI.SYMBOL
55

Portion of Batch	⅟₁	⅕	⅙	⅙	⅑
Calories	1929	386	321	321	214
Protein (g)	187	36	31	31	21
Fat (g)	121	24	20	20	13
Carbohydrates (g)	22	4	4	4	2
Fiber (g)	6	1	1	1	0.5

Gravad Lax

Curing salmon is a very simple process that will enable you to keep the fish in the fridge for a few weeks. Spicy vegetables, or aromatic bulgur, complement *gravlax* really nicely—forget about the *hovmästarsås*—the classic Swedish mustard-dill sauce. You can also add the *gravlax* to a nice and filling salad, with either wheat berries or quinoa. I cure my salmon the easiest way possible, with white pepper and lemon peel, so that I can combine it with many other flavors. You can also dill-cure it the traditional way, but it won't leave as many possibilities for variation.

2.2 lbs (1 kg) salmon fillet with skin
⅕ cup (60 g) salt
⅕ cup (42 g) sugar
1 tbsp white peppercorns, crushed in a mortar
1 lemon, the peel (grated)

Weigh the piece of salmon that you want to cure, and adjust the amount of salt and sugar according to the weight. That's usually easier than trying to cut a piece that weighs exactly 2.2 pounds. Cut the salmon fillet in half so that you get two pieces that you can place against each other. Mix salt, sugar, pepper, lemon peel, and sprinkle over one of the salmon pieces. Place the second piece on top, skin-side up. Transfer the salmon to a plastic bag, try to squeeze all the air out of the bag, and seal it. Place the bag into another bag to make sure that it doesn't leak.

Place the salmon package on a plate, and cover with a plate on top to put a little bit of pressure on top of the salmon. If you want, you can even place a weight on top. Leave the salmon at room temperature for a few hours so that the sugar and salt dissolve. Then transfer to the fridge, and let it stand there for 24 hours. Turn the salmon package a few times. Some people like their salmon thoroughly cured. If you are one of those folks, leave the salmon in the fridge for up to 48 hours. Personally, I prefer to take it out a little bit earlier, after about 18 hours. Taste your way to what suits you.

Once the salmon is cured, remove the liquid and dry off any spices before serving it.

TIP: Instead of slicing the *gravlax* thinly the traditional way, you can vary this recipe by cutting it into fairly thick slices (about 0.4 inches thick), and sauté them rapidly in olive oil at a fairly high heat. Simple and delicious!

Portion of Batch	1/1	1/5	1/6	1/6	1/10
Calories	2021	404	337	337	202
Protein (g)	184	37	31	31	18
Fat (g)	120	24	20	20	12
Carbohydrates (g)	52	10	9	9	5
Fiber (g)	0.5	0	0	0	0

With Warm Beet Salad (p. 103), and Tart Black Quinoa (p. 142).

Quick Cured Salmon with Lime and Ginger

This is one of my personal favorites, perhaps because it contains all the things I love: salmon, lime, and ginger. Best of all, it only takes a few minutes to throw together. You can eat this salmon as an appetizer, main course, or snack, but preferably, you shouldn't store it in the fridge for more than a few days. This salmon tastes great with Ill-green Sauce (page 144), but it is also very flavorful on its own.

1.1 lbs (500 g) salmon fillet, with skin
1 lime, the juice and the peel
2 tbsp ginger, grated (about 1 oz / 30 g)
flake salt
freshly ground white pepper
⅕–⅖ cup (50–100 ml) olive oil

Slice the salmon thinly, and remove the skin. You can place the salmon in the freezer for an hour before you do this to ease the process. Layer the salmon with the other ingredients, preferably in a plastic container that you can seal. Each layer: salmon slices, lime peel, ginger, salt, and white pepper. Sprinkle each layer with a little bit of lime juice and olive oil. Continue layering the salmon like this until you have used up all the ingredients. Allow to stand for 15 minutes, or up to one hour in the fridge before you serve it.

CAMILLA'S COMMENT: You'll get plenty of healthy omega-3 acids with this dish. The ginger will speed up your metabolism, and contains plenty of antioxidants. Lime contains the antioxidant vitamin C, which also stimulates the body's ability to take up iron. Remember to freeze the salmon at—0.4 degrees for at least 72 hours before you cure it, to kill any possible bacteria and parasites. That rule applies to any fish that you intend to eat raw, or cured.

Portion of Batch	● ⅟₁	● ⅕	● ⅙	● ⅕	● ⅐
Calories	1660	332	277	332	237
Protein (g)	93	19	16	19	13
Fat (g)	125	25	21	25	18
Carbohydrates (g)	40	8	7	8	6
Fiber (g)	8	1.5	1	1.5	1

With Grilled Fennel (p. 116), and wild rice.

Speedy Salmon with Coconut & Jalapeño

This speedy salmon recipe has saved me many times when I've had little time to prepare dinner. One minute in the microwave, and it's done! Add some rice, and you'll have a lovely meal. It is perfect to prepare as a lunch box, and then cook it in the microwave at work. This recipe is for one serving, and you can easily adjust how much salmon you need, according to the serving sizes in the table below. If you want to cook more than two servings of salmon simultaneously, you should divide it into rounds, and increase the cooking time in the microwave.

1 serving salmon (thinly sliced)	1 tsp honey
1 green jalapeño	1 tbsp olive oil
1 garlic clove	1 tsp flake salt
½ lemon, the juice	1 tbsp shredded coconut

Place the salmon in a microwave-safe plastic container with a tightly sealed lid. Clean the seeds from the jalapeno, and peel the garlic clove. Finely chop them, and crush them in a mortar. Pour the mix, together with the lemon juice, into the plastic container, and turn the salmon slices so that they are thoroughly covered in the seasoning. Drizzle with honey and olive oil. Sprinkle some flake salt and shredded coconut on top, and seal the plastic container with the lid. Cook in the microwave for one minute at 500 watts. If you have already made the Coconut Pesto with Green Chili (page 152), you can just use a few tablespoons of it together with a tablespoon of lemon juice, and a teaspoon of honey. Serve immediately.

TIP: You have the option to flavor the salmon with 1 tablespoon Rapeseed Oil with Fresh Turmeric (page 150), 1 tablespoon lemon juice, 1 teaspoon salt, and a little bit of black pepper. Turn the salmon in the seasoning, and prepare as above.

CAMILLA'S COMMENT: Salmon contains healthy fatty acids that protect the heart. Sometimes, farmed fish tends to be more polluted, so make sure to vary between farmed and wild-caught fish. Jalapeño is spicy , and will speed up your metabolism.

	3.5 oz salmon 100 g	5.3 oz salmon 150 g	6.2 oz salmon 175 g	7 oz salmon 200 g	8 oz salmon 225 g
Portion of Batch	1/1	1/1	1/1	1/1	1/1
Calories	372	462	508	553	598
Protein (g)	19	29	33	38	42
Fat (g)	28	34	37	40	43
Carbohydrates (g)	10	10	10	10	10
Fiber (g)	1	1	1	1	1

With Tomato & Mango Salsa (p. 109).

Thyme Cooked Baltic Herring

When you get home from work in the evening, do you find it hard to prepare a lunch box for the following day? Well, here is a delicious Baltic herring that you can easily prepare during the commercial breaks of your favorite TV show. The table below gives you nutritional values for various servings so that you can figure out which one suits your needs best. You may want to cook an extra portion while you are at it, since Baltic herring can be stored in the fridge for several days.

1 serving Baltic herring fillets	**1 tsp thyme**
½ tsp coarse sat	**1 allspice peppercorn**
1 tsp flaxseed oil	**2 white peppercorns**
1 bay leaf	**½ lemon, the juice**

First commercial break: Place the fish in a plastic bowl with salt, oil, and a crumbled bay leaf. If you are using dried thyme, crumble it into the oil as well. Crush the peppercorns in a mortar, add, and mix well. Marinate the fish for about 10 minutes.

Second commercial break: Cover the bottom of a plastic container (with a tightly sealed lid) with the marinated fish. Stand them up, side by side, so that you only see the backs. Squeeze lemon juice over. If you are using fresh thyme instead of dried, now is the time to spread it over the fish. Seal with a lid, and cook in the microwave for 5 minutes at 500 watts.

Third commercial break: Transfer the Baltic herring to the fridge. If you wish, place a pot of rice to cook on the stove. Don't forget to set your egg timer.

Allow the fish to cool. It tastes best cold with warm rice. If you made more than one serving, wait until the fish is cold before you transfer your lunch portion to a lunch box. Bring rice in a separate container that can be reheated in the microwave.

15

	3.5 oz Baltic herring 100 g	5.3 oz Baltic herring 150 g	6.2 oz Baltic herring 175 g	7 oz Baltic herring 200 g	8 oz Baltic herring 225 g
Portion of Batch	¹⁄₁	¹⁄₁	¹⁄₁	¹⁄₁	¹⁄₁
Calories	222	322	372	421	471
Protein (g)	22	33	38	44	49
Fat (g)	13	19	22	25	28
Carbohydrates (g)	6	6	6	6	6
Fiber (g)	0	0	0	0	0

With Red Raw Food (p. 104).

Baltic Herring Gratin with Feta Cheese

This Baltic herring box doesn't take more than a few minutes to prepare. The oven does the rest of the work for you. Despite the inexpensive nature of Baltic herring, this is quite a festive meal that will impress your guests. Try serving it with Red Raw Food (page 104). If you enjoy strong flavors, be generous with the feta cheese, garlic, and the anchovies.

17.5 oz (500 g) Baltic herring fillets
12 anchovy fillets with a little bit of the oil from the can
1 garlic clove, pressed or chopped
1 tbsp Dijon mustard
1 tsp salt
freshly ground black pepper
1 cup plain cooking yogurt
2 tbsp milk
3.5 oz (100 g) feta cheese, crumbled

Preheat the oven to 400 degrees. Roll the Baltic herring fillets, and place them in an ovenproof dish, dorsal fin facing up. Coarsely chop the anchovy fillets, and mix them with remaining ingredients in a bowl. Pour the mix over the fillets. Place the fillets in the top part of the oven for 25 minutes.

When you serve the fillets on the table, you can drizzle a little bit of olive oil over them, and sprinkle with some freshly ground black pepper.

CAMILLA'S COMMENT: This recipe is an inexpensive way to get important omega-3 fatty acids. Baltic fish may contain high levels of dioxin, PCB, and mercury, so you shouldn't eat such fish more than once a week. Choose fish from the Arctic Ocean, farm raised salmon, or other options for your other seafood meals. Women who want to become pregnant, who are pregnant, or who are breast-feeding shouldn't eat fish from the Baltic, or lake fish more than two to three times a year.

Portion of Batch	1/1	1/4	1/5	1/5	1/8
Calories	1596	399	319	319	200
Protein (g)	119	30	24	24	15
Fat (g)	118	30	24	24	15
Carbohydrates (g)	16	4	3	3	2
Fiber (g)	0	0	0	0	0

Coconut Fried Cod

You can use frozen cod (back) if you allow it to thaw. You can also use codfish fillets, or other firm white fish, such as Pollock, blue grenadier, or European sea bass. Different, but just as delicious, is to use chicken fillet instead. In the table below, you'll find the serving sizes in grams.

1 serving cod
2 tbsp coconut pesto with green chili (p. 152)
2 tbsp neutral oil, i.e. corn oil

Cut the fish, or chicken, into thin slices, less than 0.2 inches thick. Turn the slices in about a tablespoon of the coconut pesto, and get as much as possible to stick. Fry for two minutes at high heat, or until the pieces are cooked. Carefully turn the slices when you cook them, so that the coconut pesto doesn't fall off. Serve on plates, and spread the remaining pesto over the fish.

CAMILLA'S COMMENT: Cod is super healthy, but remember to choose eco-labeled fish. Codfish is very lean, so choose a more calorie-rich carbohydrate source, or a filling vegetable dish to serve with it.

	3.5 oz cod (100 g)	5.3 oz cod (150 g)	6.2 oz cod (175 g)	7 oz cod (200 g)	8 oz cod (225 g)
Portion of Batch	⅟₁	⅟₁	⅟₁	⅟₁	⅟₁
Calories	386	424	443	462	480
Protein (g)	17	27	30	34	38
Fat (g)	34	35	35	35.5	35.5
Carbohydrates (g)	3	3	3	3	3
Fiber (g)	1	1	1	1	1

With Golden Rice (p. 130) and Black pepper Beans Cooked in the Microwave (p. 120).

Sea Bass Gratin with Ajvar Relish

You can replace the sea bass with any other white fish that is fairly firm, such as blue grenadier, cod, pollock, or pangasius fillets. This recipe is for one serving, but the table below will give you the nutritional information depending on the weight of the fish.

1 serving white fish, i.e. sea bass
2 tsp olive oil
1 tsp lemon juice
1 pinch of fennel seeds
1 pinch of salt
2 tbsp Ajvar relish, mild
freshly ground white pepper

Preheat the oven to 400 degrees. If you're only cooking one serving, you can do it directly on the serving plate, just make sure that it is ovenproof. Otherwise, use an oven dish.

Brush the fish with olive oil, and sprinkle with some lemon juice. Use a mortar to crush the fennel seeds together with the salt. Distribute over the fillets. Spread ajvar relish over the fish until it is covered, and bake in the oven for about 10 minutes. Season with white pepper when you remove the fish from the oven.

CAMILLA'S COMMENT: Make sure that you buy Atlantic sea bass, so that you don't need to worry about heavy metals and other pollutants.

	3.5 oz sea bass	5.3 oz sea bass	6.2 oz sea bass	7 oz sea bass	8 oz sea bass
	(100 g)	(150 g)	(175 g)	(200 g)	(225 g)
Portion of Batch	⅐	⅐	⅐	⅐	⅐
Calories	197	240	261	283	304
Protein (g)	20	30	35	40	45
Fat (g)	12	12	12	12	12.5
Carbohydrates (g)	2.5	2.5	2.5	2.5	2.5
Fiber (g)	1	1	1	1	1

Quick Steamed European Plaice

This is another recipe for the microwave that you can cook directly in your lunch box. However, the result is so mouthwatering that you may want to invite guests over for a festive treat. The nutritional values below are calculated for one serving, and just like with any of the recipes where you are using the microwave, you can't cook huge quantities of food simultaneously. If you are cooking more than two servings, you should cook the fish in two batches. Also keep in mind that you may need to adjust the cooking time—a larger quantity of fish may need another 30 seconds to cook.

1 serving European plaice fillets
1 bunch of baby spinach
grated nutmeg
1 tsp lemon juice
2 tsp olive oil
freshly ground black pepper
flake salt

Place the spinach in a microwave-safe plastic container with a tightly sealed lid. Sprinkle with some freshly grated (or already ground) nutmeg. Place a fish fillet on top of the spinach, and pour lemon juice and olive oil on top. Sprinkle with black pepper and flake salt. Cook in the microwave for 90 seconds at 500 watts. Serve on plates.

CAMILLA'S COMMENT: European plaice is a lean source of protein. Always choose an eco-labeled kind, because just like cod, it is threatened by overfishing. Spinach gives you a health boost with iron, vitamin C, folic acid, and plenty of fiber. You can choose an energy-rich carbohydrate dish, or a filling vegetable dish to serve with the lean plaice.

	3.5 oz plaice	5.3 oz plaice	6.2 oz plaice	7 oz plaice	8 oz plaice
	(100 g)	(150 g)	(175 g)	(200 g)	(225 g)
Portion of Batch	½	½	½	½	½
Calories	185	231	254	276	299
Protein (g)	21	32	37	43	48
Fat (g)	11	11	11	11	11.5
Carbohydrates (g)	0.5	0.5	0.5	0.5	0.5
Fiber (g)	0	0	0	0	0

Stew with Leftovers & Kimchi

This stew is excellent when you have leftover vegetables, meat, and fish. You can buy mixed vegetable *kimchi* at Asian food markets, or you can make it yourself according to the recipe on page 88.

Meat, chicken, shrimp, fish, or octopus. Example:
  7 oz (200 g) pork tenderloin
  7 oz (200 g) octopus
  3.5 oz (100 g) shrimp
Fresh vegetables, cut into large pieces, example:
  5.3 oz (150 g) portabella mushroom

5.3 oz (150 g) green beans, whole
7 oz (200 g) cauliflower
2 garlic cloves, pressed or sliced
2 tbsp oil, preferably peanut oil
3 ²/₅ cups (800 ml) bouillon (strong)
7 oz (200 g) *kimchi* (with mixed vegetables)

Sauté the meats, vegetables, and garlic in oil at high heat for about 5 minutes. If possible, use a pot with a thick bottom that you can use to fry the ingredients. Otherwise, use a skillet and transfer the vegetables and the various meats to a pot once they are fried.

Add the bouillon, bring to a boil, and cook for about 3–4 minutes. Add fish, octopus, shrimp, and boil for another 3–4 minutes. Mix the *kimchi* into the stew right before you serve it.

Other vegetables that you can use: white cabbage, savoy cabbage, broccoli, zucchini, eggplant, onion, leek, fennel, and carrots. Serve with rice, quinoa, wheat berries, or bulgur wheat.

CAMILLA'S COMMENT: This is a very filling protein-rich dish that also contains a whole lot of carbohydrates. Therefore, you only need to serve it with a small carbohydrate addition, or skip it entirely, and add more vegetables.

GI · SAY IT OUT **40**

Portion of Batch	⅟₁	⅓	⅓	⅓	¼
Calories	1044	348	348	348	261
Protein (g)	108	36	36	36	27
Fat (g)	42	14	14	14	10.5
Carbohydrates (g)	51	17	17	17	13
Fiber (g)	18	6	6	6	4.5

Classic Roast Beef

Roast beef is great when you want to load your fridge, and lunch boxes, with protein. You can eat it warm, or cold from the fridge. Use the microwave to reheat it, or sauté it sliced or cubed. All you need is a meat thermometer, which only costs a few bucks. Without the thermometer, it is difficult to cook the roast beef exactly the way you want it. It may be difficult to find a roast beef that weighs less than 2.2 pounds (1 kg), but the bigger it is, the more succulent it will turn out. The smaller ones may turn out too dry. If you buy a large roast beef, it may take a little bit longer to bake in the oven, but everything else remains the same.

2.2 lbs (1 kg) roast beef   **olive oil**

There are several ways to make roast beef, but here are three variations that require different cooking times.

1. Preheat the oven to 250 degrees. Sauté the roast beef in a skillet, turning it so that the entire surface gets a nice color. Insert a meat thermometer into the thickest part of the roast beef, and transfer it to the oven in a sheet pan. If you want the meat rare/bloody in the middle, bake it for about 1 hour and 15 minutes, if you want it pink in the center, cook it for about an hour and a half.

2. Heat the oven to 350 degrees. Brush the roast beef with olive oil, and transfer it to the oven on a sheet pan. Don't forget to stick a meat thermometer into the thickest part of the meat. Count on at least 50 minutes per 2.2 pounds (1 kg) of roast beef, if you want the meat rare/bloody in the center.

3. Place the roast beef in a microwave-safe dish, and cook it in the microwave at maximum heat for 12 minutes. Take it out, season with salt and pepper, and cook it for another 10 minutes at full heat. You can't use the meat thermometer in the microwave, which makes it difficult to know how well done the meat gets.

Roasting the meat at low heat yields the best result. It will turn out juicier, and beautifully pink all the way through. It is also easier to keep the center temperature in check when cooking it slowly. If you are cooking the meat at a very high heat, it is paramount that you remove the meat from the oven at the exact right moment, so that it doesn't get over-cooked.

It is important to wrap the meat in aluminum foil after you remove it from the oven, and keep it covered for at least 20 minutes. Then the meat juice will settle nicely in the roast beef and make it more succulent. If you start cutting the meat too early, the meat juice will escape and make the roast beef dry.

Remember that the meat will continue to cook for a while in its own heat after you take it out of the oven, especially if you cooked it at a very high heat.

I usually aim for 134.6–136.4 degrees. Meat that is a little bit bloody will taste better when you reheat it in the skillet, or the microwave. Using the meat thermometer, you can choose how well done you want the meat. 131 degrees = rare, 140 degrees = medium, 158 degrees = well done.

CAMILLA'S COMMENT:
This is a very sufficient protein and iron boost. Roast beef is an excellent choice for people that work out.

Portion of Batch	$\frac{1}{1}$	$\frac{1}{3}$	$\frac{1}{4}$	$\frac{1}{4}$	$\frac{1}{5}$
	●	●	●	●	●
Calories	1180	393	295	295	236
Protein (g)	212	71	53	53	42
Fat (g)	36	12	9	9	7
Carbohydrates (g)	0	0	0	0	0
Fibrer (g)	0	0	0	0	0

Traditional Lamb Steak

Cooking lamb steak is easy, and it is just as practical to keep in the fridge as roast beef. You can eat it cold, lukewarm, or hot, and you always have the option to reheat it. I'm especially fond of cutting the steak into thick slices when it is cold, and reheating them in the frying pan with a little bit of oil and butter.

Lamb steak is not as lean as roast beef, so it doesn't run the same risk of drying out. That's why I tend to roast the lamb at high heat. Just like with roast beef, salmon, or chicken fillets, you'll benefit from using the meat thermometer when you cook it. Once you reach 149 degrees, the meat is rare, at 158 degrees it is medium, and at 167 degrees it is well done.

3.3 lbs (1 ½ kg) lamb steak   optional: 4 garlic cloves

Preheat the oven to 350 degrees. Use a little knife to make incisions in the meat where you can stick the garlic cloves. Stick the meat thermometer as close to the center of the steak as possible. Transfer the lamb steak to the oven in a sheet pan. Count on roasting it for about 1 hour and 45 minutes, or 2 hours if you want the meat well done (158–167 degrees). Cover the meat with aluminum foil once you remove it from the oven to keep it juicier.

CAMILLA'S COMMENT:
Another great boost of iron and protein. If you find the servings too large, you can make them smaller and serve them with a rich carbohydrate, or vegetable dish.

Portion of Batch	$\frac{1}{1}$	$\frac{1}{5}$	$\frac{1}{7}$	$\frac{1}{7}$	$\frac{1}{10}$
	●	●	●	●	●
Calories	2008	402	287	287	201
Protein (g)	298	60	42	42	30
Fat (g)	89	18	13	13	9
Carbohydrates (g)	4	1	0.5	0.5	0
Fiber (g)	0	0	0	0	0

Oven Roasted Pork Tenderloin

This is an excellent way to cook pork tenderloin, making it juicy and practical to reheat in the microwave. I usually cut it into serving sizes right away, so they look like little stumps. You also have the option to cook smaller quantities the same way.

One delicious way to cook pork tenderloin is to make an incision lengthwise, and fill it with a delicious filling. Think spicy tamarind paste, red pesto, pesto with red jalapeño, tahini pesto, or coconut pesto. The possibilities are unlimited.

2 pork tenderloins, about 2.2 lbs (1 kg)
1 tbsp olive oil
1 tbsp butter

Preheat the oven to 350 degrees. Sauté the pork tenderloins in a skillet (whole, or serving sizes), and turn them to make sure that they get a nice browned surface all around, even the short ends. Transfer the meat to a sheet pan in the center of the oven. If you can, use a meat thermometer that you stick into the center of a piece of meat. After about 20 minutes, the meat thermometer will have reached about 149 degrees. That's when you remove the meat from the oven, and cover it with aluminum foil. Leave it covered for about 15 minutes.

Tip: The quickest way to cook pork tenderloin is to steam it in the microwave. Cut it into thin slices and cook at highest heat for about 2 minutes. You can flavor it with a little bit of Tamarind Paste (page 158) and a teaspoon of oil, or with oil and Red Jalapeño Pesto (page 152).

CAMILLA'S COMMENT: The pork tenderloin is packed with protein, and like with any red meat, it is packed with iron. It is an excellent choice if you work out.

	○	◔	●	●	●
Portion of Batch	⅟₁	¼	⅕	¼	⅙
Calories	1309	327	261	327	218
Protein (g)	206	51	41	51	34
Fat (g)	53	13	11	13	8
Carbohydrates (g)	0	0	0	0	0
Fiber (g)	0	0	0	0	0

Vegetables

Stir-Frying Vegetables

You really only need to learn one way to cook your vegetables—stir-frying them in a wok. It ensures unlimited possibilities to vary your vegetable dishes. Many of the sauces and salsas in the chapter on flavor additions can be used to flavor the vegetables in the wok, or served on the side. Pretty much any vegetable can be stir-fried. You don't even need a wok. A skillet will do perfectly fine.

There are two basic principles behind stir-frying vegetables. The first one is to keep the cooking time short, because the ingredients are cooked at a very high heat while being stirred continuously. Then, you add a little bit of liquid that quickly turns into steam in the hot skillet. First you fry the food, then you steam it lightly. That is the secret behind the delicious flavor of stir-fried vegetables. They get a nice surface and flavor from being fried in the oil, and a lovely, soft texture from the steam, without getting overcooked. The short cooking time also ensures that vitamins and nutrients stay intact.

The second principle is that different vegetables and other ingredients can easily be combined as long as you adjust the cooking time and the size of the pieces. Produce that has a denser, more compact texture, such as meat and chicken, should therefore be shredded finely, while fish and shrimp should be cooked in larger pieces in the wok, towards the end of the cooking time. Vegetables that usually require more cooking time, such as carrots, beets, and other root vegetables, should be cut into thin strips, while softer veggies, such as zucchini, should be cooked in thicker pieces.

You can divide the ingredients into three groups, based on their cooking time in the wok.

Group One: Onions, potatoes, carrots, and other root vegetables, cut into thin slices or strips. White cabbage or savoy cabbage should be cut into pieces or strips that are about 0.4 inch thick. Chicken, pork tenderloin, and beef should be cut into slices or pieces that are about 0.2 inch thick. This group needs to cook about 5–6 minutes in the wok at high heat, plus an additional few minutes in the steam bath.

Group Two: Cauliflower or broccoli florets, zucchini (0.4-inch-thick slices), green beans, bell peppers (cut into pieces), fennel (slices/strips that are about 0.4 inches thick), thinly shredded white cabbage, red cabbage, or savoy cabbage. Octopus, most fish, chicken, pork tenderloin, and beef if thinly sliced (such as shreds of roast beef, chicken fillet slices that are about 0.8–1.2 inches thick). This group needs about 2–4 minutes in the wok at high heat, and then a few more minutes in the steam.

Group Three: Spinach and other leafy greens, bean sprouts, snow peas, green beans, tomatoes, bell peppers (thinly sliced), shrimp, and mussels. This group of produce can be eaten pretty much as it is, so it should only get heated. Fry them for 1–2 minutes at high heat, but you can also add them right before you add the liquid, so that you only give them a quick steam.

The skillet/wok: It is a bonus if you have access to a wok, whether it is electric, or an authentic Asian wok that you can use on a gas stove. There are also many wok pans that have a flat bottom that can be used on an electric stove, or stovetop.

However, you can also use a large skillet, preferably with a lid, but it isn't necessary. When I wok large quantities of food, I tend to use a pot to complement the cooking process. Then I fry the food at a very high heat in the skillet, and once the food has a nice browned surface after a few minutes (depending on what the produce is), I transfer it to the pot, and seal with a lid to keep it warm. Then I fill the frying pan with the next load of food and continue to cook this way until everything is done. That's when I transfer the pot to a hot plate, and add the liquid. I seal with a lid, and reheat everything for a few minutes. It won't produce the same powerful steam effect as the wok, but the result will nevertheless be delicious.

Cutting the vegetables: Cooking vegetables can be fun and easy if you learn how to cut them properly. It takes a little bit of practice, and a chef's knife. Study the photo on the next page.

The knife blade should be large so that your fist doesn't hit the cutting board when you are cutting with it. The tip of the blade should rest against the cutting board the entire time. It is of paramount importance to focus on the hand that is holding the vegetable (the left hand for most people), keep the fingers curled in, so that the knife can rest against the knuckles, or the finger joints. The left hand is responsible for feeding the vegetable under the knife—which should only be moving up and down.

This technique is the only safe way to cut vegetables without cutting your fingers, so practice it from the beginning. By supporting the knife blade with your finger joints, you are in control of the cutting process, and the thickness of the vegetables that you cut. If you learn how to easily cut vegetables into even pieces—whether they are 0.08 inch or 0.4 inch thick—you have come a long way.

Most knives have to be maintained with a knife sharpener. A sharpening tool is not expensive, and the staff at the hardware store will show you how to use it. According to a saying, the knife is sufficiently sharp when you can cut through the thin peel of a ripe tomato without any problems. However, if the blade begins to compress the tomato instead of cutting through it, the knife needs to be sharpened.

The steaming process: You can add one or two tablespoons of water to the vegetables to get a nice steaming effect. However, you can make the vegetables even tastier by using a liquid that will add flavor to the vegetables. You can use lemon juice, lime juice, orange juice, any kind of soy sauce, fish sauce, oyster sauce, tiger sauce, wine, fortified wine, vinegar, rice vinegar, sweet chili sauce, Worcestershire sauce, HP sauce, or any other type of liquid. There are countless sauces that you can buy ready at the grocery store, and in this book we have included tips on how to flavor soy sauce and use it in the wok (pages 146–147).

Combine the vegetables: Below, you will find a typical wok recipe. You can create your own recipes just as easily. Choose vegetables that look good, and that are reasonably priced. Try to keep two things in mind. First, the plate always looks more appetizing when it is filled with different colors. Colorful vegetables also contain a lot of minerals, antioxidants, and trace elements, which makes them an excellent choice from a nutritional perspective. The other thing to think about is not using too many veggies that are similar in taste. White cabbage, savoy cabbage, and napa cabbage would be quite dull together, because they all taste very similar to each other. Especially when it comes to various types of leek plants and cabbages, they tend to be very similar in taste. Always try to only use one type of cabbage, one type of onion/leek, and at least one vegetable that isn't green (i.e. carrot, beet, bell pepper, tomato, bean sprouts, red cabbage).

Wok Vegetables

Vegetables from the wok are delicious on their own, but you can always expand the meal by adding thin slices of chicken or meat. If you want to add fish, you should wait a few minutes, because it has a very short cooking time (approximately 3 minutes). You can also add shrimp or mussels at the last minute, just before you add the steaming liquid. Serve with rice or bulgur, and you'll have a complete meal.

1 carrot
10.5 oz (300 g) savoy cabbage
1 red onion
1 red bell pepper
2 tbsp corn oil
1 tbsp soy sauce
1 tbsp fish sauce
2 tbsp sweet chili sauce

Rinse and peel the vegetables. Cut the carrot into slices that are about 0.1 inch thick. To make it easier, cut off a thin slice lengthwise before you begin, so that the carrot lies still on the cutting board. Cut the savoy cabbage into shreds that are about 0.12–0.16 inch wide. Cut the onion in half, and cut each half into 3 or 4 pieces that are attached at the root. Cut the pepper in half, and remove the seeds. Cut each half into 4 pieces, lengthwise.

Heat corn oil in a frying pan/wok. Add the onion, and turn it a few times, then add the carrot slices, the pepper pieces, and the savoy cabbage at the end. Keep turning the vegetables continuously. After about 5–6 minutes, add the soy sauce and the fish sauce. Allow the liquid to evaporate. It takes about a minute or so. Lower the heat, and cover with a lid. Allow to stand and settle for a minute, before you add sweet chili sauce.

CAMILLA'S COMMENT: Carrots and cabbage are both packed with important antioxidants, and some of those healthy nutrients become available during the cooking process.

GI · 54 TOTAL

	●	●	●	●	●
Portion of Batch	1/1	1/3	1/3	1/3	1/4
Calories	511	170	170	170	128
Protein (g)	10	3	3	3	2.5
Fat (g)	31	10	10	10	8
Carbohydrates (g)	45	15	15	15	11
Fiber (g)	11	4	4	4	3

Sesame Fried Vegetables

Use a mandoline to quickly cut the vegetables into beautiful strips. This is the first dish I cooked when I bought a mandoline, and it is still one of my favorites. The sesame flavor goes well with root vegetables, and it will turn any meal into a luxurious treat.

1 ¾ lbs (800 g) vegetables, and root vegetables, example:
1 large beet
1 parsnip
1 large carrot
1 zucchini
2 potatoes
2 tbsp sesame oil
2 tbsp fish sauce
1 lime, the juice
1 tbsp olive oil
1 tbsp butter

Peel the beet and the parsnip. If the carrot and the potatoes have a thin peel, it's enough to scrub them, otherwise you should peel them too. Use a mandoline, or a knife, to cut the vegetables into strips that are about 0.12–0.16 inch wide. Mix the vegetable strips with sesame oil, fish sauce, and the fresh squeezed lime juice.

Fry for 4–5 minutes at medium heat in butter and oil. If your skillet isn't very large, you should fry the vegetables in two batches. If you want to serve all of it simultaneously, return the first batch of vegetables to the pan when everything is fried, and reheat everything.

CAMILLA'S COMMENT: A large serving of this vegetable dish will have you covered with all the carbohydrates you need during a meal. A smaller serving can be combined with an additional carbohydrate dish. It is packed with vitamins, antioxidants, and other nutrients. Keep in mind that the GI value is lower for the individual serving than for the entire batch.

Portion of Batch	⅟₁	¼	¼	¼	⅕
Calories	636	159	159	159	127
Protein (g)	13	3	3	3	2.5
Fat (g)	28	7	7	7	5.5
Carbohydrates (g)	74	19	19	19	15
Fiber (g)	16	4	4	4	3

With Oven Roasted Pork Tenderloin (p. 76).

Traditional Kimchi

Kimchi is a national dish of Korea, and rightfully so. The lightly smoked, mild chili flavor can get anyone hooked. *Kimchi* can be served as an appetizer, or as a side dish. It is the main flavor ingredient in Stew with Leftovers & *Kimchi* (page 74). You can mix all kinds of vegetables, but try using white cabbage as the main ingredient because it is both healthy and inexpensive.

about 2.2 lbs (1 kg) vegetables, i.e. white cabbage, carrots, beets, parsnip, napa cabbage, savoy cabbage, daikon, radishes

⅓ cup (90 g) salt
85 oz (2 ½ l) water
1 piece of fresh ginger (1.75 oz / 50 g) peeled, and finely shredded

2 garlic cloves, peeled, finely chopped
1 red chili fruit, cored, and sliced
⅖–⅗ cup (95–150 ml) kimchi sauce

Cut up the vegetables using a mandolin. It's a quick and easy way to cut them into thin rods. Add the salt to the water and soak the vegetables. Place a plate, or something similar, on top to keep all the vegetables underneath the water. Store cold for at least 12 hours.

Pour out the water, and add ginger, garlic, chili, and the *kimchi* sauce. Store in a tightly sealed container in the fridge for at least a week. One trick to start the lacto-fermentation process is to take one teaspoon of liquid from any other lacto-fermented vegetables, and add it to your *kimchi* to speed up the formation of healthy bacteria. Otherwise, it will happen on its own, it will just take a little bit longer. Try waiting a few weeks before you eat your *kimchi*, even though it should be ready to eat within a week.

It is very important to use thoroughly cleaned jars and tools, and have clean hands, when preparing *kimchi* to make it possible to store for several weeks without any added preservatives, or heat treatment.

CAMILLA'S COMMENT: I love *kimchi*, and could eat it for lunch and dinner every day. Good thing it is super healthy: the lacto-fermentation creates healthy pro-biotic bacteria, which aid digestion and the immune system. The lacto-fermentation process preserves vitamins, antioxidants, and other nutrients in the vegetables, and it lowers the GI value of the entire meal.

GI • SYMBOL **55**

	●	●	●	●	●
Portion of Batch	⅟₁	¼	¼	¼	⅙
Calories	620	155	155	155	103
Protein (g)	29	7	7	7	5
Fat (g)	3	1	1	1	0.5
Carbohydrates (g)	114	29	29	29	19
Fiber (g)	28	7	7	7	5

Quick Kimchi with White Cabbage

According to the traditional *kimchi* recipe, the vegetables should stand in the kimchi sauce for a week or longer. However, you can also heat the white cabbage in the microwave for a few minutes if you want to cook a speedy version. The microwave will turn the cabbage a little bit soft, albeit still crispy, and it brings out the sweetness of the cabbage. Ready to eat in just a few minutes.

21 oz (600 g) white cabbage
2 tsp lemon juice
1 tsp salt
2 tsp neutral cooking oil
3 tbsp *kimchi* sauce

Carefully slice the cabbage into strips that are about 0.8 inch wide. Then cut those pieces across, so that you get pieces that are about 0.8 x 1.2 inches. Transfer the cabbage to a plastic container. Add lemon juice, salt, and cooking oil. Cover with a lid and lightly shake the container to distribute the liquid over the cabbage, then heat in the microwave (with the lid on) for 2 minutes. Add the *kimchi* sauce and shake the container again. You can eat this cabbage lukewarm or cold, and it can be stored in the fridge for several days.

CAMILLA'S COMMENT: White cabbage contains vitamins and antioxidants like vitamin C, vitamin E, and beta-carotene. Thanks to the mild cooking process, the beta-carotene becomes more available to the body.

GI · SYMBOL **25** TOTAL

Portion of Batch	⅛	⅓	⅓	⅓	⅓
Calories	390	130	130	130	130
Protein (g)	9	3	3	3	3
Fat (g)	23	8	8	8	8
Carbohydrates (g)	32	11	11	11	11
Fiber (g)	12	4	4	4	4

Quick Steamed Golden Vegetables

Steaming vegetables in the microwave is simple and healthy. They may be the best option for a lunch box, as there is barely any preparation involved. Feel free to combine these veggies with the recipe for the microwave-cooked salmon, or Pork tenderloin (page 62 and 78, respectively), and serve with some rice or bulgur.

1 small parsnip (about 2.5 oz / 70 g)
1 small carrot (about 3.5 oz / 100 g)
1 piece of white cabbage (about 3.2 oz / 90 g)
1 tsp fish sauce
1 tsp freshly squeezed lemon or lime juice
1 tbsp Rapeseed Oil with Fresh Turmeric (page 150)
optional: a pinch of salt

Rinse and shred vegetables, and transfer them to a plastic container with a tightly sealed lid. Add the remaining ingredients, and shake thoroughly to distribute all the ingredients evenly. Cook at highest setting in the microwave for 2 minutes. The cooking time will vary slightly depending on the thickness of your shredded vegetables, so check on them after 2 minutes, and cook them for an additional 1 and a half minutes if necessary. Preferably, the vegetables should remain a little bit crispy, but it is up to you how soft or crisp you like them.

CAMILLA'S COMMENT: Plenty of vitamins, antioxidants, and other nutrients, and best of all, they become available to our body because of the light cooking process. The GI value will vary with the serving size, so the individual portion has a lower GI number than the entire batch.

GI · SYMBOL **80**

Portion of Batch	1/1	1/2	1/2	1/2	1/2
Calories	213	107	107	107	107
Protein (g)	4	2	2	2	2
Fat (g)	11	5.5	5.5	5.5	5.5
Carbohydrates (g)	22	11	11	11	11
Fiber (g)	7	3.5	3.5	3.5	3.5

With Quick *Kimchi* with White Cabbage (p. 89) on the right, and Traditional *Kimchi* (p. 88) in the front.

Grilled White Cabbage

This recipe proves that you can do pretty much anything with white cabbage. If you have a mandoline, this dish won't take more than a few minutes to prepare, plus the 10 minutes on the grill. The lemon peel cuts the sweetness of the cabbage nicely with a hint of bitter citrus flavor. If you don't like the bitterness of it, you can either lessen the amount of lemon peel, or leave it out completely.

3 tbsp olive oil
1.1 lbs (500 g) white cabbage
3 garlic cloves, pressed
optional: ½ lemon, finely grated zest
freshly ground black pepper
1 tsp salt, preferably herb salt
½–1 tsp chili flakes

Preheat the oven to 500 degrees on the grill setting. Brush a baking sheet with some of the olive oil. Finely shred the white cabbage, directly over the sheet if you wish. Pour garlic, lemon, spices, and olive oil over the cabbage, and use your fingers to distribute everything evenly. Grill in the middle of the oven for 5 minutes. Take out, and turn the cabbage around, and grill for another 5 minutes. The cabbage is as delicious hot as cold.

CAMILLA'S COMMENT: White cabbage is super healthy, and contains high levels of vitamin C, vitamin E, and vitamin K, as well as beta-carotene, and folic acid. In addition, it is packed with minerals: magnesium, calcium, and potassium. Chili increases thermogenesis.

Portion of Batch	⅓	¼	¼	¼	¼
Calories	555	139	139	139	139
Protein (g)	8	2	2	2	2
Fat (g)	46	12	12	12	12
Carbohydrates (g)	24	6	6	6	6
Fibrer (g)	10	2.5	2.5	2.5	2.5

With Oven Roasted Pork Tenderloin (p. 78), and
Grilled Garlic (p. 160).

Hot Green Beans

If you wish to keep your carbohydrate intake low, green beans are an excellent choice because they can replace rice or potatoes. If you don't count your carbohydrates, you can serve these green beans as a veggie side. You can pretty much eat as much as your heart desires, because they are super healthy. I tend to cook 2.2 pounds (1 kg) while I'm at it, because they go very quickly. I snack on these beans like candy—they are just as delicious when served cold the following day.

2.2 lbs (1 kg) green beans, fresh or
    frozen
2 tsp salt
3 tbsp water
4 tbsp olive oil
2 garlic cloves, finely chopped

10–20 anchovy fillets, finely chopped
⁴/₅ cup (appr. 100 g) black olives, with
    or without the pits
2 tbsp grated lemon zest
1 tsp chili flakes

Preheat the oven to 500 degrees on the grill setting. Heat the beans in the microwave for 2 minutes at the highest setting, together with the salt and the water. It is important that you use a plastic container with a lid. If you don't have one that is big enough to hold all of the beans, heat them in rounds.

Pour out the water, and transfer the green beans to a baking sheet. Pour the remaining ingredients over the beans, and mix well with thoroughly clean hands.

Grill in the middle of the oven for about 20 minutes. Take them out after half of the cooking time, turn the beans, and return to the oven.

CAMILLA'S COMMENT: Beans are packed with nutrients on their own, and with the olives, they get a boost of healthy fats. Choose olives that are authentically black, avoid the kinds with artificial color added. Read the packaging thoroughly, and don't buy any olives that contain E numbers.

GI · SYMBOL 32

	●	●	●	●	●
Portion of Batch	⅟₁	⅛	⅛	⅛	⅟₁₀
Calories	1238	155	155	155	124
Protein (g)	35	4.5	4.5	4.5	3.5
Fat (g)	93	12	12	12	9
Carbohydrates (g)	46	6	6	6	5
Fiber (g)	44	5.5	5.5	5.5	4

With Baked Salmon (p. 56).

Stir-Fried Cauliflower with Ginger & Chili

Cauliflower tastes delicious when combined with strong flavors. I like it best when it is crispy, so I try to keep the cooking time as short as possible. Then it stays fresh even when you reheat it.

1 medium size cauliflower (about 28 oz / 800 g)
1 medium size ginger root (about 1.8 oz / 50 g)
1 red chili (the larger variety, mild)
2 tbsp peanut oil
1 tbsp water
1 tsp soy sauce
1 tbsp fish sauce

Use a knife to cut out the stem from underneath. You only need to make an incision, so that you can break the stem off. Do the same thing with the pieces. Make an incision so that you can break the florets apart until you are happy with their size. Peel the ginger, cut it in half lengthwise, and slice it thinly. Split the chili, and remove the seeds and the white part. Cut it into fine strips. Heat the peanut oil in a skillet. Sauté the cauliflower, the chili, and the ginger at the highest heat for 1–2 minutes. Use a spatula to turn the food often to prevent the chili and the ginger from getting burned at the bottom of the pan. Add water, soy sauce, and fish sauce. This will give the cauliflower a nice steam. Allow most of the liquid to evaporate—it takes about 1–2 minutes.

CAMILLA'S COMMENT: Ginger and chili speed up the metabolism, and they have anti-inflammatory properties. Cauliflower is rich in iron and vitamin C. It is also an excellent choice from an environmental perspective, because of its outdoor cultivation and the option to buy it locally produced.

Portion of Batch	1/1	1/4	1/4	1/4	1/4
Calories	555	139	139	139	139
Protein (g)	16	4	4	4	4
Fat (g)	32	8	8	8	8
Carbohydrates (g)	43	11	11	11	11
Fiber (g)	21	5	5	5	5

Grilled Savoy Cabbage

Savoy cabbage has an aromatic flavor that adds a nice touch to your cooking. It is excellent with fish, chicken, and meat.

1 savoy cabbage (about 2.2 lbs / 1 kg)
olive oil, or rapeseed oil

Preheat the oven to 400 degrees on the grill setting. Cut the cabbage in half at the root, then cut each half into three wedges that are attached to each other at the base. Transfer them to a tightly sealed plastic container, and heat in the microwave for 2 minutes at the highest setting. Divide the pieces into two batches if you can't fit all of them into the same container. You also have the option to cook them in boiling water for 1 minute, instead of using the microwave. Spread the cabbage over a baking sheet that has been brushed with olive oil, or covered with parchment paper. Brush the cabbage with olive oil. Grill for 10 minutes in the top part of the oven. Remove the cabbage from the oven, turn it, brush the other side with olive oil, and grill for another 5–10 minutes.

TIP: You can grill cauliflower the same way, but then you'll need to preheat the oven to 450 degrees on the grill setting. You don't need to boil or microwave the cauliflower before you grill it.

CAMILLA'S COMMENT: Cabbage is packed with iron, calcium, vitamin C, and beta-carotene. It is also rich in fiber, and contains glucosinolates—organic compounds that are broken down to antioxidants during digestion.

GI · SYMBOL
40

Portion of Batch	⅟₁	¼	¼	¼	¼
Calories	678	169	169	169	169
Protein (g)	20	5	5	5	5
Fat (g)	50	12.5	12.5	12.5	12.5
Carbohydrates (g)	36	9	9	9	9
Fiber (g)	25	6	6	6	6

Chickpea Stew from North Africa

In North Africa, couscous (la semoule in French) is a type of chickpea stew that you eat with the tiny grains. They have a pretty high GI value, which is great if you want to build muscle mass. If you want to lower the GI, you can serve this stew with bulgur, quinoa, or only use half of the couscous and complement the other half with bulgur or quinoa. That way, you still get the traditional flavor, but a lower GI.

2 yellow onions
1.1 lbs (500 g) raw chorizo
2.2 lbs (1 kg) chicken thigh fillets
3 garlic cloves, peeled
⅕ cup (50 ml) olive oil
3 bay leaves
2 allspice peppercorns
10 black peppercorns
1 tbsp salt
2 tbsp tomato purée
1 tsp chili paste (can be replaced with a pinch of chili powder, or chili flakes)
68 (2 l) oz water
5 tbsp liquid veal fond/bouillon, or chicken fond/bouillon
1 small savoy cabbage (about 26.5 oz / 750 g), can be replaced with white cabbage
3 medium size carrots (about 14 oz / 400 g)
2 firm zucchinis (about 25 oz / 700 g)
3 cans chickpeas (already cooked) (3 x 14 oz / 400 g) together with the liquid
⅕ cup (50 ml) Rapeseed Oil with Fresh Turmeric (page 150), can be replaced with 2 tbsp dried turmeric sautéed in 3 tbsp rapeseed oil

Peel the onions, and cut each into 8 wedges that are attached at the root. Sauté chorizo, chicken, garlic, and onion in olive oil in a large cast iron pot, or a skillet, until the ingredients have a nice color. Transfer the ingredients to a large pot, or into two pots if necessary.

Add the spices, salt, tomato purée, chili paste, water, and veal fond. Cut the savoy cabbage into six wedges that are attached at the base. Peel or scrub the carrots. Cut the carrots and zucchinis into large pieces. Add the vegetables to the pot, bring to a boil, and cook for 20 minutes. Add the chickpeas, and cook for a few more minutes. Add the rapeseed oil with the turmeric, and stir.

This stew will feed 10–12 people, and it can be stored in the fridge for at least 10 days. You can reheat it, and use it for your lunch boxes. You can expand this stew by adding more meat if you happen to have leftovers of roast beef, pork tenderloin, or chicken, and you can add more bouillon if necessary. This stew is at its best a few days after you cook it.

he serving sizes are calculated by taking into
onsideration that you would eat this stew
ith a serving of carbohydrates, and an addi-
onal vegetable dish. However, you can eat
ore of the stew instead, and lessen the car-
ohydrate portion or skip it entirely, and just
dd another vegetable serving if you wish. If
ou want to make the stew richer in carbo-
ydrates and proteins, add more chickpeas.

	●	●	●	●	●
Portion of Batch	1⁄1	1⁄14	1⁄18	1⁄18	1⁄20
Calories	5603	400	311	311	280
Protein (g)	396	28	22	22	20
Fat (g)	283	20	16	16	14
Carbohydrates (g)	321	23	18	18	16
Fiber (g)	115	8	6	6	6

GI · SYMBOL
50

101

Pink Coleslaw

The beet gives this coleslaw a beautiful color, and the apple makes it nice and tart.

1 parsnip, optional: a piece of celeriac (about 3.5 oz / 100 g)
10.5 oz (300 g) white cabbage
1 large beet
1 large carrot
1 firm red apple
⁴/₅ cup (2 dl) plain cooking yogurt
2 tsp French mustard
²/₅ cup (1 dl) mayonnaise
2 tsp salt
1 tsp fennel seeds

Coarsely grate the parsnip, and shred the white cabbage as finely as you can. Transfer to a plastic container with a lid, and heat in the microwave at 500 watts for 30 seconds. Peel and grate the beet and the carrot. Grate the apple, together with the peel. Combine with the remaining ingredients. If you can, lightly crush the fennel seeds in a mortar before you add them—it will bring out their flavor. You can also rub them between your fingers before you combine them with the other ingredients.

CAMILLA'S COMMENT: This is an energy-rich side with plenty of delicious nutrients, such as folic acid, iron, magnesium, vitamin K, vitamin C, beta-carotene, and quercetin (an antioxidant). The selection of root vegetables and veggies in this recipe are all good environmental choices because they are cultivated outdoors, and can be produced locally most of the year.

GI · SYMBOL 55

	⬤	⬤	⬤	⬤	⬤
Portion of Batch	¹/₁	1/8	1/8	¹/₁₀	¹/₁₀
Calories	1145	143	143	115	115
Protein (g)	15	2	2	1.5	1.5
Fat (g)	95	12	12	9.5	9.5
Carbohydrates (g)	60	7.5	7.5	6	6
Fiber (g)	14	2	2	1.5	1.5

Warm Beet Salad

Just like carrots, beets have a nice sweetness to them. They are easy to get a hold of year-round, but are at their prime during the fall, when they come straight from the ground to the store. You can fry the stalks in butter, together with a little bit of crushed garlic, and grated lemon peel—a delicacy!

2–3 beets
1 tbsp water
⁴/₅ cup (appr. 200 ml) Anchovy dressing (page 162)

Peel the beets and cut them into bite-sized pieces. In a plastic container with a tightly sealed lid, heat the pieces with the water in the microwave for 3 minutes at 500 watts. Let them cool for a minute or so before you stir in the dressing. If you don't have time to prepare the anchovy dressing, you can add a few tablespoons of olive oil or linseed oil, juice from half a lemon, a crushed garlic clove, and some salt and pepper.

CAMILLA'S COMMENT: Beets contain lots of minerals, among them calcium and iron, and they are packed with vitamin C.

			●	●	●	
Portion of Batch	⅟₁	1/3	1/3	1/3	1/4	
Calories	466	155	155	155	117	
Protein (g)	21	7	7	7	5	
Fat (g)	19	6	6	6	5	
Carbohydrates (g)	57	19	19	19	14	
Fiber (g)	14	5	5	5	3.5	

Red Raw Food

Sometimes one plus one equals three, and that is certainly true for this recipe. Despite the use of very simple ingredients, this salad is plenty flavorful. The sweet root vegetables meet with zesty citrus, salt, and linseed oil. Yum!

2–3 beets (about 7 oz / 200 g)
1–2 carrots (about 7 oz / 200 g)
½ tsp salt
2 tbsp linseed oil
2 tbsp freshly squeezed lemon juice

Peel carrots and beets. Grate them coarsely. Combine with remaining ingredients, and preferably store in the fridge before serving this salad. It is delicious with almost anything, but mouthwatering with Baltic herring.

CAMILLA'S COMMENT: This is a boost of vitamins, antioxidants, and fibers, in a delicious, beautiful, and healthier format than supplement pills. The GI will vary depending on the serving size, meaning it will be lower for an individual serving than for the entire batch.

GI · SYMBOL

86

	●	●	●	●	●
Portion of Batch	⅟₁	1/3	1/3	1/4	1/4
Calories	454	151	151	114	114
Protein (g)	5	1.5	1.5	1	1
Fat (g)	31	10	10	8	8
Carbohydrates (g)	37	12	12	9	9
Fiber (g)	10	3	3	2.5	2.5

With Pink Coleslaw (p. 102) on the left, and
Warm Beet Salad (p. 103) in the back.

Spinach Salad with Almonds and Orange Dressing

I learned this recipe at my friends' house in Montreal. It is so simple that I retained it in my memory immediately, and I make it every time spinach is in season. You can use spinach in any salad that calls for leafy greens or lettuce. Make sure that the dressing contains a zesty element, such as vinegar or lemon juice. Let the spinach soak in the dressing for a few minutes—the acidity will soften the greens a bit. A spinach salad is both filling and nutritious.

1.1 lbs (500 g) spinach
2 oz (60 g) sliced almonds
²/₅ cup (about 100 ml) freshly squeezed orange juice

²/₅ cup (100 g) plain cooking yogurt
½ tsp salt

This salad is really delicious if you use freshly harvested spinach. You can find baby spinach (tender baby leaves of spinach that have been harvested early) in most stores year-round. It is a good alternative, but doesn't have as much flavor as the fresh spinach. Real leaf spinach needs to be thoroughly rinsed in cold water. Not only to clean it, but the water also makes the spinach crispy. Try soaking it in cold water for 10 minutes, or longer. Cut, or break off, the leaves from the stalks. Tear the leaves into bite-sized pieces. Place the trimmed spinach in a colander to get rid of excess water.

Roast the sliced almonds in a dry, clean skillet at medium heat. Watch them carefully, so they don't burn. Shake the frying pan to turn the almond slices. Mix the freshly squeezed orange with the yogurt. Season with salt. Mix the spinach in the dressing. Sprinkle with the almonds.

CAMILLA'S COMMENT: Spinach is full of iron, vitamin C, beta-carotene, Q-10, and vitamin E. One serving of spinach provides you with half of the recommended value of magnesium and potassium, and more than a third of the daily recommended value of calcium. In addition, it contains plenty of fiber. Almonds contain healthy fats. If the leaf spinach makes you gassy, use the baby spinach instead.

GI · SYMBOL **49**

Portion of Batch	⅓	1/4	1/4	1/4	1/4
Calories	544	136	136	136	136
Protein (g)	23	6	6	6	6
Fat (g)	29	7	7	7	7
Carbohydrates (g)	27	7	7	7	7
Fiber (g)	10	3	3	3	3

Green Mango Salad

Ripe mango is delicious for dessert, or as a complement to chicken or salmon. But sometimes, you'll come home and cut up the mango to discover that it isn't ripe. I save the situation by making this salad—it tastes best with unripe mango. However, you also have the option to make it with ripe mango.

1 large mango (about 13 oz / 365 g)
optional: 1 small red chili, or chili flakes
1 pinch of flake salt
1 lime, the juice
0.5 oz (15 g) dry roasted peanuts

Peel the mango, and use a knife to release the fruit from the pit. Slice the mango thinly. Cut the chili into skinny slices. Combine mango, chili, salt, and lime juice. Preferably store it cold for a while. Crush the peanuts in a mortar, and sprinkle over the salad right before you serve it. If you don't have fresh chili at home, you can sprinkle some chili flakes over the salad instead.

CAMILLA'S COMMENT: Mango is packed with vitamin A and vitamin C, and it is an excellent source of vitamin B6 and fiber. Chili and lime give an additional vitamin-C boost, and the peanuts—which are actually legumes, and not nuts—contain several vitamins and healthy fats.

GI · SYMBOL
73

Portion of Batch	⅟₁	1/2	1/2	1/2	1/3
Calories	298	149	149	149	99
Protein (g)	6	3	3	3	2
Fat (g)	8	4	4	4	2.5
Carbohydrates (g)	47	24	24	24	16
Fiber (g)	6	3	3	3	2

Tomato & Mango Salsa

This salsa will turn out delicious whether the mango is ripe, green, or in between. Tasty with salmon, tuna, chicken, or as a little side dish.

1 large mango (about 13 oz / 365 g)
4 firm tomatoes, preferably plum tomatoes
½ small red onion
1 lime or lemon, the juice
1 tsp flake salt, or ½ tsp salt
freshly ground white pepper

Peel the mango, and use a knife to loosen the fruit from the pit. Cut the mango into pieces, or cubes. Do the same to the tomatoes. Peel and chop the red onion. Combine mango, tomatoes, and onion. Add lime juice, salt, and pepper.

CAMILLA'S COMMENT: This salad provides you with plenty of vitamin A, vitamin C, folic acid, fiber, and the antioxidant, lycopene.

	●	●	●	●	●
Portion of Batch	⅓	1/2	1/2	1/2	1/3
Calories	304	152	152	152	101
Protein (g)	5	2.5	2.5	2.5	1.5
Fat (g)	1	0.5	0.5	0.5	0
Carbohydrates (g)	62	31	31	31	21
Fiber (g)	10	5	5	5	3

GI • SYMBY 58 TO

The Best Tomato Salad

At a restaurant on Lamu, an island along the coast of Kenya, I ate a fantastic tomato salad. I asked the owner, and chef, how he prepared it. I thought I misunderstood him at first. Could it be possible that tomatoes, bell peppers, onion, and lemon juice could make such a delicious combination? No secret ingredient, or spice? Finally, he took me back to the kitchen and showed me himself how he prepared it. This salad tastes absolutely amazing, even though it is so simple, and fat free.

3–4 firm tomatoes (about 14 oz / 400 g)
1 large green pepper (about 7 oz / 200 g)
1 large red onion (about 7 oz / 200 g)
1 lemon, the juice
½–1 tsp salt

This salad tastes best when served cold, so it is beneficial if the ingredients are straight from the fridge when you begin chopping them up.

Cut tomatoes, pepper, and onion as thin as you can (0.03–0.04 inch). Use a mandoline for the pepper and onion to make it easy. You'll need to cut the tomatoes by hand, as they may get crushed in the mandoline. Squeeze the lemon. Combine vegetables, lemon juice, and ½ teaspoon of salt. Season with more salt if necessary.

CAMILLA'S COMMENT: This salad is a pure antioxidant and vitamin boost: lycopene, vitamin C, B1, B6, folic acid, vitamin E, and plenty of healthy trace elements.

Portion of Batch	⅛	1/2	1/2	1/2	1/2
Calories	217	109	109	109	109
Protein (g)	8	4	4	4	4
Fat (g)	1	0.5	0.5	0.5	0.5
Carbohydrates (g)	41	20.5	20.5	20.5	20.5
Fiber (g)	11.5	6	6	6	6

16 GI · SYMBOL

With Green Mango Salad (p. 108) in the background, and
Tomato & Mango Salsa (p. 109) in the front.

Two Minutes until Mealtime

Tomatoes soften as soon as they ripen. I invented this recipe because I didn't want to throw out another half-empty box of tomatoes that weren't one hundred percent fresh. Soft tomatoes are excellent for making sauce. Preferably, use cocktail or plum tomatoes. Regular tomatoes are usually too watery in taste.

8.8 oz (250 g) tomatoes
1 tbsp olive oil
1 tbsp fish sauce
1 garlic clove, pressed
1 pinch of chili flakes
2 tbsp butter
1.8 oz (50 g) ädelost, 30% (Swedish blue cheese)

Cut each tomato into 4 wedges, or large pieces. If you are using cocktail tomatoes, it's enough to make a hole with a fork (otherwise they will explode in the microwave). Cook the tomatoes and the remaining ingredients in the microwave at highest setting for 2 minutes.

Serve with pasta (see the nutrition table on page 34 for various serving sizes for the pasta).

CAMILLA'S COMMENT: The portion sizes can be problematic for the person who is trying to get more defined (a lot of fat, little protein), and the person who is aiming for weight loss (a lot of fat). In that case, you may want to adjust the amount of butter and ädelost, the serving size of the pasta, and perhaps only eat a salad with this meal to balance it out. Or at least make sure to get the daily intake balanced.

Portion of Batch	⅟₁	1/2	1/2	1/2	1/3
Calories	616	308	308	308	205
Protein (g)	15	7.5	7.5	7.5	5
Fat (g)	55	27.5	27.5	27.5	11
Carbohydrates (g)	14	7	7	7	4.5
Fiber (g)	0	0	0	0	0

GI · SYMBOL **62** TOTAL

Roasted Red Pepper

Roasted peppers are deliciously flavorful, and excellent as a side. Best of all, you can store them in olive oil in the fridge for several weeks. I take the opportunity to stock up when peppers are inexpensive, that is usually when they are at their best—ripe and sweet.

10 large red bell peppers (about 3 lbs / 1.4 kg)
3 garlic cloves
³⁄₅ cup (150 ml) olive oil
1 lemon, the juice
optional: thyme, preferably fresh
salt
freshly ground black pepper

Preheat the oven to 500 degrees on the grill setting. Cut the peppers in half, lengthwise, and remove the seeds. Place the peppers, peel side up, on a baking sheet that has been brushed with oil or been covered with parchment paper. Grill in the upper part of the oven for about 25 minutes. The peel should turn black (at least spots of black), and begin to crack. Remove the baking sheet from the oven and transfer the peppers to a tightly sealed plastic container, or plastic bag. Leave them in there for 10 minutes, then you will be able to remove the peel easily with a knife. Cut each half into two or three pieces. Peel the garlic, and slice it thinly. Layer peppers, lemon juice, garlic slices, spices, and olive oil in a plastic container. The pepper should almost be entirely covered in the oil and lemon juice.
      Store in the fridge, and serve with meat, fish, or chicken.

CAMILLA'S COMMENT: Red peppers are rich in vitamin C, vitamin E, beta-carotene, and several B vitamins. Thanks to the cooking process, the beta-carotene becomes more available to the body.

	○	○	●	●	●
Portion of Batch	⅟₁	⅟₁₀	⅟₁₀	⅟₁₅	⅟₁₅
Calories	1684	168	168	112	112
Protein (g)	16	2	2	1	1
Fat (g)	138	14	14	9	9
Carbohydrates (g)	85	8.5	8.5	6	6
Fiber (g)	27	3	3	2	2

Roasted Eggplant

This side, with its distinct Italian flavors, tastes delicious with pretty much anything. A little bit of roasted eggplant will turn any sandwich with roast beef, chicken, or cheese into a festive meal. Can be served warm straight from the oven, or cold; you can store it in the fridge for several weeks.

3 medium size eggplants
olive oil
salt
3 garlic cloves
optional: fresh thyme
²/₅ cup (100 ml) balsamic vinegar

Preheat the oven to 350 degrees. Rinse the eggplant, and cut off the green stalk. Cut them lengthwise into slices that are about 0.2 inch wide. If you are having a hard time cutting through the peel, you may need to sharpen your knife. Cut the slices in half, diagonally. Brush a baking sheet with olive oil. Spread the eggplant slices over the sheet, and brush them with olive oil. Sprinkle lightly with salt. Grill for 10 minutes in the upper part of the oven (fairly high up). Remove from the oven, turn the eggplant slices, and lightly salt the other side. Return them to the oven, and grill for 10 more minutes. Peel the garlic, and slice it thinly. Layer eggplant, garlic, thyme, salt, balsamic vinegar, and olive oil in a plastic container with a tightly fitted lid. Continue to layer until you run out of eggplant and garlic. The eggplant slices should pretty much be covered in olive oil and balsamic vinegar.

CAMILLA'S COMMENT: Eggplant contains a lot of folic acid, calcium, selenium, and beta-carotene—which becomes more available to the body through the cooking process.

Portion of Batch	½₁	1/8	1/8	¹/₁₀	¹/₁₀
Calories	1149	144	188	115	115
Protein (g)	15	2	2	2	2
Fat (g)	91	11	11	9	9
Carbohydrates (g)	55	7	7	6	6
Fiber (g)	30	4	4	3	3

Grilled Fennel

Grilled vegetables have a rich, luxurious flavor. And they pretty much cook themselves, while you prepare the rest of the meal. Fennel is excellent with fish, chicken, and meat. Also check out the recipe for the Roasted eggplant (page 115).

2 fennel bulbs (about 10.5 oz /300 g each)
olive oil
salt

Preheat the oven to 500 degrees on the grill setting. Brush an oven sheet with olive oil. Slice the fennel (max 0.2 inch wide), and make sure that they stay attached at the base, the rhizome. Spread them over the oven sheet, and brush with olive oil. Salt lightly, and place high up in the oven. Turn the fennel after 15 minutes, and grill for 10 minutes, or until the slices look golden and crispy around the edges. Can be stored in the fridge for a few days, and can be eaten cold, or reheated in the microwave.

Portion of Batch	⅟₁	1/4	1/4	1/4	1/6
Calories	613	153	153	153	103
Protein (g)	17	4	4	4	3
Fat (g)	52	13	13	13	9
Carbohydrates (g)	11	3	3	3	2
Fiber (g)	20	5	5	5	3

With Poached Cold Salmon (p. 57), Tapenade (p. 163),
Roasted Red Pepper (p. 114), and Roasted Eggplant (p. 115).

Fennel Salad with Pear & Walnuts

You'll benefit from using a mandoline when making this salad, because the fennel and pear need to be sliced very thinly. A little bit of salt will bring out the licorice tones of the fennel, which creates a nice contrast against the sweet pear.

1 fennel (about 10.5 oz / 300 g)
1 tsp salt
1 large, firm pear (about 10.5 oz/ 300 g)
½ lime
1 tsp sugar
2 tsp linseed oil
1.8 oz (50 g) walnuts
1 tbsp olive oil
flake salt

Slice the fennel very thinly, preferably with a mandoline, but don't forget to wear the finger protection. Mix the fennel with the salt, and place a weight on top. You can use a stone or metal mortar, or a deep plate or bowl, and place a milk carton on top. Cut the pear in half, remove the core, and slice thinly. Squeeze the lime. Combine the pear slices with the sugar, olive oil, and the lime juice. Chop the walnuts and roast them in olive oil in a frying pan, at medium heat. Turn them constantly, to prevent them from getting burned. Sprinkle with flake salt.

The fennel will soften from the salt after about 15 minutes. Pour out the liquid, and rinse the fennel with cold water in a colander. Drain for a few minutes. Mix the fennel with the pear slices, and garnish with the walnuts.

CAMILLA'S COMMENT: The serving sizes will remain pretty small if you don't want the calorie value too high. If you are going to eat a larger portion, try to combine with a smaller serving of the carbohydrate and protein complements.

	○	○	●	●	●
Portion of Batch	⅟₁	1/4	1/5	1/5	1/5
Calories	794	199	159	159	159
Protein (g)	16	4	3	3	3
Fat (g)	57	14	11	11	11
Carbohydrates (g)	49	12	10	10	10
Fiber (g)	22	5.5	4	4	4

Black Pepper Beans Cooked in the Microwave

This is another dish that only takes a few seconds to throw together. Perfect when you don't have much time to prepare your lunch box. If you have access to fresh green beans, they taste the best. However, this recipe was intended for frozen beans. Just like all the other microwave recipes in this book, the nutritional value is calculated based on an individual serving that would be good for your lunch box. You can make larger batches by doubling the ingredients, but keep in mind that the microwave isn't as effective with larger quantities of food. You can cook up to two servings simultaneously. If you are making more than that, you will need to divide the beans and cook in several batches.

frozen green beans (about 5.3 oz / 150 g)
1 tbsp Santa Maria Black Pepper Sauce (or another favorite Tex Mex sauce)
1 tsp neutral oil, i.e. corn oil
1 pinch of flake salt.

Put all the ingredients in a plastic container, and seal with a tightly fitted lid. Shake the container thoroughly until the sauce is distributed over all the green beans. Heat at highest setting in the microwave for 3 minutes. A double portion of the beans can replace a carbohydrate option, such as rice or bulgur, especially if you wish to lower your carbohydrate intake or eat fewer calories.

TIP: This recipe also works with shredded carrots, shredded white cabbage, or a blend of both. Heat for 2 minutes, and check if they are cooked. Usually, carrots and cabbage take less time to cook than frozen green beans.

CAMILLA'S COMMENT: Green beans contain plenty of vitamin E, vitamin C, and several B vitamins—such as folic acid. They are also rich in selenium, iron, calcium, and potassium. Mild microwave cooking will preserve the vitamins.

	●	●	●	●	●	
Portion of Batch	⅟₁	⅟₁	⅟₁	⅟₁	⅟₁	
Calories	130	130	130	130	130	
Protein (g)	3	3	3	3	3	
Fat (g)	8	8	8	8	8	
Carbohydrates (g)	9	9	9	9	9	
Fiber (g)	5	5	5	5	5	

GI · SAVORY **42** ABOUT

Carbohydrates

Pasta with Avocado Sauce

There are hundreds of different kinds of pasta in Italy. They all have different names—the Italians take their pasta very seriously and carefully pair their pasta with selected sauces. You don't need to be quite as picky, but this sauce won't go as well with egg pasta, such as *tagliatelle* or *pappardelle*, which have a slightly doughy texture. Penne, bow pasta, or any of the traditional kinds made with durum wheat flour will go perfectly with this sauce. Or, use whole grain pasta if you prefer that.

1.1 lbs (500 g) pasta
2 avocados (about 10.5 oz / 300 g)
2 tbsp olive oil
1 tsp salt
½ tsp freshly ground black pepper
1 tsp ground coriander

⅗ cup (150 ml) cooking cream
optional: ⅕ cup (50 ml) milk, 2%
optional: parmesan, or pecorino (grated)
optional: parsley

Heat the pasta water. Cut the avocado in half, and remove the pit. Chop the avocado, and use a fork to mash it. You can also mix it in a blender. Slice the garlic very thinly, and sauté it in olive oil at low or medium heat, until it gets a nice color. Season with salt, pepper, and coriander. Add the cooking cream, and simmer for a few minutes.

Cook the pasta according to the instructions on the packaging. Be careful not to overcook it. It is better to stop cooking it a minute too early. Pasta with a little bit of chewing resistance has a lower GI, and can be reheated without becoming too boring.

Stir the mashed avocado into the garlic cream, and allow it to get warm. Dilute it with a little bit of milk if the consistency gets too thick. Stir the sauce into the freshly cooked pasta. Serve with freshly grated parmesan, or pecorino if you want. You also have the option to cut some fresh parsley on top.

CAMILLA'S COMMENT: This is almost a complete meal, but I recommend an additional portion of protein and vegetables for people that work out at an intense level.

	●	●	●	●	●
Portion of Batch	⅟₁	1/4	1/5	1/5	1/6
Calories	2743	686	549	549	457
Protein (g)	67	17	13	13	11
Fat (g)	99	25	20	20	16.5
Carbohydrates (g)	381	95	76	76	63.5
Fiber (g)	24	6	5	5	4

Farmer Pasta

This is probably the simplest way to quickly make a pasta dish. At least if you have some leftover pasta in the fridge. This recipe is suitable for one or two servings, so if you are going to cook more, you may not fit all the food in the skillet. It is better to cook it in several batches if making more than two servings.

1 tbsp olive oil

1 tsp butter

1 serving cooked pasta (see nutritional value for different serving sizes, p. 32)

½ tsp sugar

1 garlic clove, pressed

1 egg

1.8 oz (50 g) parmesan or pecorino, grated

freshly ground black pepper

optional: chili powder, or chili flakes

optional: parsley

Heat a skillet with olive oil and butter to high/medium heat. Add the pasta, and sprinkle with a little bit of sugar. It will give the pasta a nice and crispy surface, and such a small amount won't affect the nutritional value, or the GI number. Turn the pasta regularly. Once it has a nice color, after about 5 minutes, add some garlic, turn it again, and fry the pasta for a minute or two more. Crack the egg directly into the pan, and stir it around. Turn off the heat almost immediately. The egg should barely have time to coagulate. Stir down the cheese into the pan, and season with black pepper. If you wish, you can also add a little bit of chili, and fresh parsley.

CAMILLA'S COMMENT: I recommend eating this dish with an additional serving of protein. It could be a pure protein source such as chicken fillet (serving size depending on your energy need), or a vegetable dish that also provides you with proteins. The egg, and the parmesan already contain quite a bit of protein. Tip: By sprinkling your meals with parmesan (or nuts, or seeds) you increase the proteins and calories in the meal—great for whoever is trying to gain weight, but has a hard time eating enough to do so.

GI · SYMBOL 68

Portion of Batch	⅟₁	⅟₁	1/2	1/2	1/2
Calories	687	687	344	344	344
Protein (g)	34	34	17	17	17
Fat (g)	41	41	21	21	21
Carbohydrates (g)	45	45	23	23	23
Fiber (g)	2	2	1	1	1

Pasta Sauce with Chicken Liver

This sauce is also excellent with rice or bulgur, but a great Italian classic with pasta. Pasta that contains egg has a lower GI value, and I usually serve this sauce with either *papardelle* or *tagliatelle*. You can replace the turkey bacon with regular bacon, but that will increase the caloric value.

8.8 oz (250 g) egg pasta, i.e. *tagliatelle*
1 package smoked turkey bacon, 6% fat (4.4 oz / 125 g)
1 yellow onion
14 oz (400 g) chicken liver
2 tbsp olive oil
2 tbsp balsamic vinegar
2 tsp Worcestershire sauce
⅖ cup (100 ml) cream, 15%
⅕ cup (50 ml) milk, 2%
1 ½ tbsp sage, dried
1 tsp salt

Cook the pasta according to the directions on the packaging. Cut the turkey bacon into pieces, and chop the onion. Fry in oil at medium heat for 5 minutes. Cut each chicken liver into 2–4 pieces. Raise the heat, and fry the liver together with the onion for 5 minutes. Add balsamic vinegar and Worcestershire sauce, and lower the heat. Simmer for a few minutes, then add the cream and milk and simmer for a minute or two. Season with sage, salt, and mix the sauce with the freshly cooked pasta.

CAMILLA'S COMMENT: This meal provides you with a lot of energy for little money. Thanks to its high iron content, chicken liver is great to eat every once in a while if you work out a lot.

GI · SYMBOL
20

Portion of Batch	⅓	1/4	1/5	1/5	1/7
Calories	1364	341	273	273	195
Protein (g)	105	26	21	21	15
Fat (g)	95	24	19	19	14
Carbohydrates (g)	31	8	6	6	4
Fiber (g)	1.5	0.5	0	0	0

Feijoada in No Time

In Brazil, *feijoada* is a festive meal. The black beans are usually cooked for several hours with all kinds of meat, and served with rice and salad. This is a 15-minute version that is made with cooked beans.

Fresh sausage refers to sausage that contains raw meat, and needs to be cooked before you eat it. Fresh *chorizo, salsiccia,* or fresh *merguez* can often be found at regular grocery stores, and they give the black beans a lovely flavor.

3 tbsp olive oil	3 cans of black beans (14 oz / 400 g each)
1 yellow onion	
2 garlic cloves	1 tsp salt
1 package bacon (5.3 oz / 150 g)	1 tsp freshly ground black pepper
3 bay leaves	optional: 1 bunch coriander, coarsely chopped
1 tsp coriander, ground	
1⅓ oz (600 g) pork tenderloin	optional: 1 pinch chili flakes
10.5 oz (300 g) fresh, spicy sausage	

Heat olive oil at medium heat in a large skillet. Chop the onion, garlic, and cut the bacon into strips. Fry together with the bay leaves and the coriander for about 5 minutes.

Cut the pork tenderloin into bite-sized pieces, and add them to the frying pan. Add the sausages whole, but if they are really big, take them out after a few minutes and cut them in half. Sauté the meat and the sausage with the onion blend for 5 minutes, and add 3 cans of black beans that have been drained in a colander. Simmer the beans with the meat. Season with salt, pepper, and if you wish, a little bit of fresh coriander and chili flakes right before you serve the meal.

CAMILLA'S COMMENT: This is a complete meal that contains proteins, carbohydrates, and fat. Just add a few vegetables to add extra vitamins, and carbohydrates.

GI · 50 ROUTES

Portion of Batch	⅟₁	1/5	1/6	1/6	1/8
Calories	3668	734	611	611	459
Protein (g)	297	59	50	50	37
Fat (g)	179	36	30	30	22
Carbohydrates (g)	222	45	37	37	28
Fiber (g)	83	17	14	14	10

Golden Rice

Just like Arborio rice, the sushi rice grains are large and firm, which gives them excellent flavor without being mushy and porridge-like. However, sushi rice is also delicious on its own, or with a little bit of soy sauce.

1 yellow onion
1 tbsp rapeseed oil
1 tsp salt
½ tsp cumin
⅘ cup (about 150 g) (can be replaced with Arborio rice, or
    regular parboiled rice)
1⅓ cup (300 ml) broth (chicken, vegetable, or meat flavored)
⅕ cup (50 ml) Rapeseed oil with turmeric (page 148)

Chop the onion, and allow it to soften in the oil together with salt and cumin. Add the rice and mix it thoroughly with the onion, and simmer for a few minutes. Add the broth and bring to a boil, then lower the heat and cover with a lid. Taste the rice after about 10–15 minutes. It shouldn't be hard in the center, but should preferably have some chewing resistance. If you choose any other type of rice than sushi rice, you will need to adjust the amount of broth according to the cooking instructions on the packaging, as different types of rice retain different amounts of liquid. The rice tastes the best if you don't allow all of the broth to cook into the rice. Add the rapeseed oil with the turmeric, and serve.

CAMILLA'S COMMENT: The GI value provided for this recipe is 69, but it will be slightly lower. Partially because of the oil with the turmeric, but also because the individual servings will have a lower GI than the entire batch. The GI value will also differ depending on the type of rice you choose.

GI · SYSTEM
69

Portion of Batch	1/1	1/3	1/4	1/4	1/6
Calories	1104	368	276	276	184
Protein (g)	17	5.5	4	4	3
Fat (g)	51	17	13	13	8.5
Carbohydrates (g)	150	50	38	38	25
Fiber (g)	6	2	1.5	1.5	1/6

Coconut Rice

This rice is heavenly delicious, and will make any meal luxurious. You can adjust the amount of coconut milk if you wish to lower the fat content. However, at least one third of the liquid should be coconut milk, otherwise you won't taste the coconut.

1 1/3 cup (about 240 g) sushi rice
1 cup (250 ml) coconut milk
3/5 (150 ml) water
1 tsp water

Various kinds of rice have different cooking times, and need different amounts of water. If you are using other types of rice than sushi rice, read the instructions on the packaging, and replace about half of the water with coconut milk. Keep in mind that coconut milk easily boils over, so heat the rice carefully, and watch it as it boils. Other than that, you cook the rice as usual.

CAMILLA'S COMMENT: Thanks to its texture, sushi rice that is cooked without the sweet traditional Japanese dressing has a lower GI value than hard, polished rice. The coconut milk adds proteins, healthy saturated fats, and a delicious flavor.

GI·SYMBOL
74

Portion of Batch	1/1	1/3	1/4	1/4	1/6
Calories	1111	370	278	278	185
Protein (g)	18.5	6	5	5	3
Fat (g)	21	7	5	5	3.5
Carbohydrates (g)	213	71	53	53	36
Fiber (g)	9	3	2	2	1.5

Spice Risotto

This recipe was inspired by a vacation to Zanzibar, where spices such as cinnamon, cardamom, and clove are often used in cooking. Pork, or chicken, is excellent with this risotto, but Grilled Chicken Thigh Fillets with Spicy Tamarind (page 40) are absolutely delicious with it.

4 cardamom pods, or ½ tsp cardamom seeds
6 whole cloves
4 allspice peppercorns
½ tsp cinnamon, ground
½ tsp caraway seeds
1 tsp salt
2 tbsp rapeseed oil
1¾ cups (400 ml) chicken broth
⁴/₅ cups (150 g) Arborio rice
optional: ²/₅ cup (about 20 g) parmesan, grated

Fry the spices in the rapeseed oil over medium heat for a few minutes. Bring the chicken broth to a boil. Add the rice to the oil, and fry it for a few minutes. Pour ⅕–²/₅ cup of the broth over the rice. Allow to boil over medium heat, then add more bouillon and continue to cook the rice this way until you have used up all the broth. During the last addition of broth, lower the heat to the lowest option or the almost lowest setting. Make sure that all of the bouillon doesn't boil away, but the risotto should have porridge-like consistency when served. Right before you serve it, you can add grated parmesan to make the risotto extra delicious.

CAMILLA'S COMMENT: This is filling, and full of heating spices (see page 180) that will speed up your metabolism. Parmesan adds extra protein and calcium.

GI · SAY
68
TO

Portion of Batch	⅟₁	1/3	1/4	1/4	1/6
Calories	1104	368	276	276	184
Protein (g)	31	10	7	7	5
Fat (g)	45	15	11	11	7.5
Carbohydrates (g)	140	47	35	35	23
Fiber (g)	2	0.5	0.5	0.5	0

With Coconut Rice (p. 131), far right, and Golden Rice (p. 130), in the background.

Berry Bulgur

Adding nuts, raisins, and goji berries will make your bulgur more fun and colorful. You have the option to leave out any of the ingredients, so even if you only have raisins and nuts at home, this bulgur will turn out delicious.

1¾ (400 ml) broth
⁴⁄₅ cup (about 110 g) whole grain bulgur
1 tbsp olive oil
1 tbsp butter
²⁄₅ cup (about 35–40 g) goji berries
²⁄₅ cup (about 35–40 g) raisins (green or yellow)
²⁄₅ cup (about 50 g) nuts, preferably walnuts, or pine nuts
optional: salt

Bring the broth and bulgur to a boil. Boil for 5 minutes, turn off the heat, and let it stand for 5 minutes. Heat a skillet at medium heat, add oil and butter, then fry the berries and the nuts for a few minutes while continuously stirring. Add the bulgur to the skillet, and mix well. Taste, and add salt if necessary. Serve out of the pan.

CAMILLA'S COMMENT: Goji berries are full of antioxidants, minerals, and vitamins. They get their red color from carotenes. Bulgur is similar to couscous, but retains more nutrients and fiber when cooked. Raisins are rich in fiber, and even the slightest addition gives a nice energy boost to your meal. Walnuts are packed with healthy polyunsaturated fats, folic acid, vitamin E, and several important minerals and fibers.

GI • 56 YOUR BODY

Portion of Batch	⅟₁	1/3	1/4	1/4	1/5
Calories	1094	365	274	274	219
Protein (g)	26	9	7	7	5
Fat (g)	53	18	13	13	11
Carbohydrates (g)	126	42	32	32	25
Fiber (g)	19	6	5	5	4

Red Bulgur

This bulgur has a rich flavor, and is so succulent that it can replace sauces and other condiments. This batch is enough for two large servings, but you can easily adjust the portions according to your energy needs, and amount of servings. Just add more bulgur, and increase the other ingredients accordingly.

²/₅ cup (about 55 g) bulgur (regular or crushed)
1 pinch of salt
⁴/₅ cup (200 ml) water
²/₅ cup (about 80 g) ajvar relish
⅕ cup (about 45 g) plain cooking yogurt
1 pinch herb salt
freshly ground black pepper

Cook the bulgur, but not according to the instructions on the box, which usually makes it overcooked. Instead, bring bulgur, salt, and water to a boil, lower the heat, and simmer for 6–7 minutes. Turn off the heat, but leave the pan on the hot plate for 5 more minutes. Pour out any excess liquid.

Add the *ajvar* relish, the yogurt, and stir. Season with herbal salt (or regular salt), and freshly ground black pepper.

CAMILLA'S COMMENT: Bulgur is rich in fiber and is filling, but if you are looking to gain greater definition, or lose weight, you will need a larger serving to feel full; you can skip the sauce/flavor addition, and choose raw food or salad as a vegetable side. Complete with a large protein serving.

	○	○	●	●	●
Portion of Batch	½	1/2	1/2	1/3	1/3
Calories	488	244	244	163	163
Protein (g)	8	4	4	3	3
Fat (g)	9	5	5	3	3
Carbohydrates (g)	35	18	18	12	12
Fiber (g)	6	3	3	2	2

Hearty Wheat Berry Salad

Wheat berries, or spelt, mixed with yogurt, grated cheese, and nuts make for a healthy, creamy blend that can be served as a cold salad at dinner, providing the meal with plenty of carbohydrates. Nowadays, you can buy ready-to-eat wheat berries in a can, so you can cut the cooking time to just a few seconds. Here, I have flavored it with mango, but you can replace it with pear, apple, pomegranate, or a shredded root vegetable, i.e. carrot or beet.

1 1/3 cup (about 310 g) wheat berries, or spelt
1 small mango (about 10.5 oz / 300 g)
1.8 oz (50 g) walnuts
1 tbsp olive oil
1 tsp salt
2/5 cup (about 100 g) plain yogurt
2/5 cup (20 g) grated parmesan
freshly ground black pepper

Cook 1 1/3 cups of wheat berries, or spelt, according to the directions on the packaging. You don't need to soak the wheat berries or spelt, even if the instructions on the box recommend it. Also keep in mind that you probably won't need to cook the grains as the instructions recommend. Check on them after about two-thirds of the time has passed. If the wheat berries have a good chewing resistance, there is no need to continue cooking them, but you can pour out the boiling water. You also have the option to use canned ready-to-eat wheat berries to save time.

Peel the mango, without cutting it in half. Coarsely grate the fruit. It won't matter if the mango isn't entirely ripe. If the mango is too soft, it may be difficult to grate. Then you can cut it with a knife and slice it thinly instead. Roast the walnuts in a frying pan with the olive oil and ½ tsp of salt over medium heat. Turn them constantly to prevent them from burning on the bottom of the pan. Combine remaining ingredients with the wheat berries, and season with black pepper and the rest of the salt.

If you want this dish to look more festive, you can save some of the cheese and nuts to add as garnish on top of this risotto right before you serve it.

TIP: A dollop of this salad with a piece of cold boiled or grilled chicken fillet makes a perfect snack, since you don't need a kitchen or a microwave to reheat it.

With Berry Bulgur (p. 134) in the center, and
Red Bulgur (p. 135) in the back, right.

CAMILLA'S COMMENT: This meal is packed with nutrients: folic acid, iron, zinc, healthy fats, calcium, and a great balance of proteins and carbohydrates. The serving sizes are calculated by taking into consideration that you are going to add a protein source and some vegetables to create a complete main course. You can easily adjust the portions, and get a great snack. The balance between the protein and carbohydrates makes this dish an excellent meal on its own, preferably with a few extra vegetables.

GI · SYMBOL 50

	●	●	●	●	●
Portion of Batch	1/1	1/5	1/6	1/6	1/8
Calories	2165	433	361	361	270
Protein (g)	66	13	11	11	8
Fat (g)	76	15	13	13	2
Carbohydrates (g)	298	60	50	50	37
Fiber (g)	53	11	9	9	7

Fake Risotto with Spelt

This is an energy-rich dish that can be stored in the fridge for a long time. I tend to make a huge batch, and keep it as the foundation for the week's lunch boxes. This also makes an excellent snack. Therefore, this recipe produces a pretty large batch, but you always have the option to halve it.

1¾ cup (295 g) spelt
⅘ cup (185 g) crème fraiche, 15%
optional: 1 tbsp French mustard
1 garlic clove

1 cup (about 150 g) black, pitted olives, preferably Kalamata olives
2 tbsp capers (about 25 g)
10–12 anchovy fillets (about 20 g)

Rinse the spelt grains, and cook them with 3 ⅓ cups (800 ml) of water and 1 teaspoon of salt. Bring to a boil, and lower the heat immediately; simmer for about 15 minutes. Sample to make sure that the grains have a nice chewing resistance, but are not too hard. Remove the pot from the heat and allow the spelt to sit in the cooking water for 5–10 minutes, after which they should be soft enough. The greater the chewing resistance, the lower the GI—ensuring that the grains won't become too mushy when you reheat them in the microwave.

Add the crème fraiche and the mustard (optional). Press a garlic clove and add it. Chop olives, capers, and anchovies as finely as you can. You can also chop them in a blender using the pulse setting, but be careful not to do it too long so that they don't turn into a smooth paste. Combine with the spelt.

This can be eaten warm, or cold, and can be stored in the fridge up to a week if kept in an airtight container.

CAMILLA'S COMMENT: The endurance training and definition portions are fairly large, but a ¼ of the batch would be too small of a serving. Adjust the serving sizes, or the protein and vegetable dishes that you eat with this dish. The olives provide you with healthy fats. Mustard is a thermogenic spice (see page 180).

GI · SYMBOL 50

Portion of Batch	½	1/3	1/3	1/3	1/5
Calories	997	332	332	332	199
Protein (g)	54	18	18	18	11
Fat (g)	93	31	31	31	19
Carbohydrates (g)	172	57	57	57	34
Fiber (g)	27	9	9	9	5

Red Onion Quinoa

This refreshing quinoa variation is just as delicious cold as it is warm, and therefore excellent in a salad or as a snack. The speed-marinated red onion can be prepared separately, and is excellent as a side with meat or fish.

2 red onions (about 7 oz / 200 g each)
2 tsp salt
2 tsp sugar
½ tsp fennel seed
½ lemon, the juice
2 tsp linseed oil
⁴/₅ cup (about 135 g) red quinoa

Slice the red onion very thinly, preferably with a mandoline. Combine with salt and sugar, and leave for about 15 minutes. Add 34 ounces (1 liter) of cold water and stir, then pour out the water using a colander. Flush the onion with water over the sink for 30 seconds, and drain the water, which will take a few minutes.

Season with fennel seeds (that you have crushed in a mortar), lemon juice, and oil. Cook the quinoa according to the directions on the packaging, but be alert. The cooking time on the box is usually longer than necessary. Just like many other types of grains, quinoa is a lot tastier, and has a lower GI value, if it isn't overcooked. Sample the quinoa after about two-thirds of the cooking time. If you think it tastes ready, pour out the water, and adjust the cooking time next time. Add the marinated onion to the quinoa. You have the option to make this dish with light or black quinoa.

CAMILLA'S COMMENT: Quinoa contains slow carbohydrates, and is the most protein-rich seed. The crop contains plenty of iron, magnesium, and zinc. In this dish, the quinoa and the linseed in the speed-marinated red onion both contain healthy fatty acids.

	●	◉	●	●	●
Portion of Batch	¹/₁	1/3	1/4	1/4	1/5
Calories	1031	344	258	258	206
Protein (g)	31	10	8	8	6
Fat (g)	20	7	5	5	3
Carbohydrates (g)	178	59	45	45	36
Fiber (g)	25	8	6	6	5

Refried Beans

Refried beans are very popular in the Mexican kitchen. The beans are boiled, and then fried so they turn into a fried bean medley. This simplified recipe can be made with canned ready-to-eat beans, and provides a powerful flavor in just a few minutes.

2 tbsp olive oil
1 yellow onion
2 garlic cloves
1 package of bacon, about 4.2 oz / 120 g
28 oz (800 g) boiled cannellini beans, black-eyed peas, borlotti beans, or
    black beans
1 tsp salt
1 tsp freshly ground black pepper
2 tsp coriander (ground), or 1 tsp cumin
2 pinches of chili flakes, or 1 tsp chili powder

Heat the olive oil in a large skillet over medium heat. Chop onion, garlic, and shred the bacon. Fry for about 5 minutes. Increase the heat and add the beans. Mash some of the beans with the spatula, and fry for a few minutes. Add the spices. The beans taste best when they are lukewarm, preferably with a dollop of plain yogurt. Speed-Marinated Red Onion Quinoa (p. 139) is also excellent with the refried beans. Beans and yogurt, combined with another vegetable, will make up a complete meal or snack. Beans are rich in proteins and carbohydrates.

CAMILLA'S COMMENT: The serving sizes are calculated so that you can add another protein source (yogurt, or anything else) and large vegetable serving to make this a main course. If you want to eat the refried beans as a snack, you will need to adjust the portions slightly.

	●	●	●	●	●
Portion of Batch	1/1	1/3	1/4	1/4	1/5
Calories	1624	541	406	406	325
Protein (g)	83	28	21	21	17
Fat (g)	78	26	19.5	19.5	16
Carbohydrates (g)	121	40	30	30	24
Fiber (g)	56	19	14	14	11

With Speed-Marinated Red Onion Quinoa (p. 139), and
Red Jalapeño Pesto (p. 152).

Tart Black Quinoa

Linseed oil makes the quinoa delicious even when it is cold, straight out of the fridge. You can use it to make a filling salad or a delicious snack. You have the option to use red or light quinoa, but I recommend the black variation, as it has more flavor.

⅘ cup (about 135 g) black quinoa
1½ cups (350 ml) water
2 tbsp fish sauce
1 tbsp light, or Japanese soy sauce
½ stalk lemongrass
1 lime, the juice
2 tbsp linseed oil

You don't need to soak the quinoa, but, other than that, follow the instructions on the package. Rinse the quinoa with hot water. Put it in a pot with water, fish sauce, soy sauce, and the lemongrass cut into two pieces. Make sure to lower the heat to the lowest possible setting as soon as the water begins to boil. Check on the quinoa when it begins to reach the end of the cooking time, and sample it to see if it has enough chewing resistance. If it is done and you still have liquid in the pot, pour the water out. Flavor with lime juice and linseed oil.

CAMILLA'S COMMENT: Black quinoa contains iron, magnesium, and zinc. It has a low GI value, and a fairly high protein content. Combine with a protein source and plenty of vegetables.

GI • LOW 33

Portion of Batch	⅟₁	⅓	¼	¼	⅕
Calories	933	311	233	233	187
Protein (g)	25	8	6	6	5
Fat (g)	38	13	10	10	8
Carbohydrates (g)	123	41	31	31	25
Fiber (g)	19	6	5	5	4

Flavor Additions

Ill-Green Sauce

This intensely tart sauce is excellent with salmon, chicken, octopus, and pork tenderloin. This batch is enough for 5–10 servings, and can be stored in the fridge for a few days. If you want it to keep longer, you should freeze it in individual servings.

2.8–3.2 oz (80–90 g) fresh coriander
2.8–3.2 oz (80–90 g) flat-leaf parsley
3/5 oz (about 150 ml) olive oil
1 ½ tsp salt
2 limes, the juice
1 garlic clove
 freshly ground black pepper
optional: 1 tsp sugar

Carefully weigh coriander and parsley, and rinse in a colander (if you begin by washing them, you won't get the correct weight since they'll retain some of the water, making them heavier). Thoroughly shake off the water.

Cut the leaves with scissors or chop them coarsely with a knife, and then mix the coriander and the parsley in a blender with the remaining ingredients until everything is thoroughly mixed—the blend begins to foam a little bit. Save some of the lime juice and the olive oil to use towards the end. That way, you can add them according to your own preference. You can add the sugar the same way, if you think it is needed. A really ripe lime has a little bit of sweetness to it, and you may not need to add the sugar at all.

Ginger Soy Sauce

Ginger is best combined with soy sauce that has a little bit of sweetness to it, such as the traditional Chinese soy sauce, which is often referred to as mushroom soy sauce. You can also combine one part sweet soy sauce with one part Japanese soy sauce, or the Chinese soy sauce that is often referred to as light soy sauce. It is thinner, not sweet at all, and is made only with soybeans. Read the ingredients list if you are unsure. If the soy sauce contains mushrooms it means it will have a slightly thicker consistency, be darker in color, and sweeter in taste.

3.5 oz (100 g) fresh ginger
$^2/_5$ cup (100 ml) Chinese mushroom soy sauce
1 tbsp fish sauce

Peel the ginger, and grate it over a bowl so that you catch all the juice. Place the grated ginger in a fine-mesh sieve, and use a spoon to press the juice out. Mix the ginger juice with soy sauce and fish sauce. This blend can be stored in the fridge for several weeks, and can be used as a flavor addition on the table, or in the wok.

Szechuan Soy Sauce

Szechuan pepper has a unique, aromatic flavor. This sauce can be used to flavor fish, chicken, pork, and meat. You can add it in the wok to flavor your vegetables, use it as a dipping sauce, or flavor lightly steamed vegetables with it. This is a great sauce to keep in the fridge, so make a double batch while you are at it.

4 tsp whole Szechuan pepper
$^1/_5$ cup (50 ml) Japanese soy sauce
$^1/_5$ cup (50 ml) balsamic vinegar
1 tbsp rapeseed oil

Crush Szechuan pepper in a mortar. Quickly bring soy sauce, vinegar, rapeseed oil, and pepper to a boil. Lower the heat, and simmer for 2 minutes. Strain through a sieve to remove the Szechuan pepper, and use a teaspoon to squeeze the remaining liquid out of the peppercorns. This sauce can be served warm, lukewarm, or cold.

Chili & Sesame Soy Sauce

This soy sauce is ridiculously simple to make, but absolutely irresistible. In China, it is common to combine sesame and chili, and it makes the chili less intense in flavor. This tastes better with soy sauce that isn't sweet. The Japanese brand, Kikkoman, is common at grocery stores and works perfectly with this sauce. Asian food markets sell light Chinese soy sauce, which is made only with soybeans (light soy sauce). There, you will also find Chinese chili sauce, which is pretty hot. That's what I usually use. If you want to use a regular, European chili sauce, you may need to add a little bit of extra chili paste or chili powder to make it a little bit spicier.

²/₅ cup (100 ml) Chinese soy sauce, or   **1 tbsp chili sauce**
Japanese soy sauce   **1 tbsp sesame oil**

Combine the ingredients in a bottle, seal it, shake it thoroughly, and store it in the fridge. You can keep this sauce for several weeks in the fridge, and you can use it to flavor rice, bulgur, meat, fish, or your wok vegetables. In the recipe on page 150, you have the option to use one or two tablespoons of this soy sauce instead of the rapeseed oil with turmeric when you steam the vegetables in the microwave.

Tamarind Soy Sauce

Various brands of tamarind concentrates come in very different strengths. Sometimes it is light in color with a fluid consistency, other times it is thick like tar, but most kinds are somewhere in between. Therefore, it is quite impossible to determine the exact quantity needed. Begin with a teaspoon, and taste to see if you need more.

²/₅ cup (100 ml) Chinese soy sauce, or   **1–2 tsp tamarind concentrate**
Japanese soy sauce   **2 tbsp fish sauce**

Pour all the ingredients into a jar, or bottle that you can seal, and store in the fridge. Shake for a minute or two, until the tamarind dissolves. This sauce can be stored for several weeks. You can use it to flavor rice, or when you stir-fry vegetables, meat, or fish in the wok.

Tamarind & Sesame Dip

This sauce will carry a piece of salmon, pork tenderloin, or chicken. You can also drizzle it over stir-fried vegetables, or use it as a dipping sauce.

4 tbsp balsamic vinegar
1 tbsp sesame oil
1 tbsp honey
1–2 tsp tamarind concentrate
½ tsp salt

Reduce the vinegar by half by simmering it over medium heat. It takes a few minutes. Carefully watch the pan, and stir, preferably with a spatula. Add the remaining ingredients, and mix thoroughly until the tamarind concentrate dissolves in the warm sauce. Simmer for 30 seconds.

Tahini Mayo

The consistency of this sesame sauce reminds me of mayonnaise. Sometimes, tahini is made from sesame seeds that have been dark roasted. That kind of tahini has a darker color, and has a more bitter taste—which doesn't complement any of my recipes. It is better if you look for a lighter tahini.

4 tbsp tahini
1 tbsp sesame oil
2 tsp rice vinegar
½ tsp salt
3 tbsp water

Combine all the ingredients, except for the water. Then add the water, by the tablespoon, and stir until you are happy with the consistency. If you store this tahini mayo in the fridge for a few days, you may need to stir it again to get the right consistency.

Rapeseed Oil with Fresh Turmeric

Fresh turmeric is a type of root that you can find at most Asian food markets. It is cheap, and worth the trouble of finding. This oil is a flavor sensation that is reminiscent of saffron, horseradish, and carrot. A teaspoon of this oil goes especially well with root vegetables, but it can also be used to flavor fish, stews, and chicken. It is included in several recipes in this book.

1.8 oz (50 g) fresh turmeric
1 cup (250 ml) cup rapeseed oil, preferably cold pressed
1 tsp salt

Clean the roots, and cut off any dry or dark parts if you see any. You don't need to peel the turmeric. Mix them in a blender, together with the oil, until they are thoroughly combined. Season with salt. This oil can be stored in the fridge for several months. Be careful when you handle turmeric, as it has a strong yellow color that can be difficult to remove from wooden utensils and plastic bowls.

If you can't get a hold of fresh turmeric anywhere, you can do the following:

Fry a small, finely chopped yellow onion in a couple tablespoons of rapeseed oil. Once the onion is transparent, add 2 tablespoons of ground turmeric and sauté for a minute or two over low heat. Transfer to a blender together with ⅗ cup (150 ml) rapeseed oil, and mix. Season with salt, approximately ½ teaspoon, and add some freshly grated horseradish, about 0.35 oz / 10 g.

Tahini Pesto

This tahini pesto has a very unique and spicy flavor. It is excellent on a piece of bread, as a dipping sauce with vegetables, or as a condiment with chicken or meat.

4 tbsp tahini   **1 tsp salt**
4 tsp *kimchi* sauce   **2 tbsp water**
4 tbsp sesame seeds   **1 tbsp rapeseed oil**

Combine all the ingredients. You can add a little bit more water if you want a looser consistency.

Coconut Pesto with Green Chili

This pesto is included in several recipes throughout this book, such as the Coconut Fried Cod (page 68). You can also serve it with fish, shellfish, or chicken. If you don't like coriander, you can replace it with flat-leaf parsley.

3.5 oz (100 g) coconut flakes
3–4 green chili peppers, preferably jalapeño (about 1.8 oz / 50 g)
2 garlic cloves (about 0.35 oz / 10 g)
1 tbsp coarse salt

1 tsp sugar
½ lemon, the juice
²/₅ cup (about 20 g) fresh coriander, chopped
2 tbsp olive oil

Remove the seeds from the chili peppers. Chop the chili together with the garlic, and transfer to a mortar. Crush the blend together with salt and sugar. Combine all the ingredients. Store in a tightly sealed container.

Red Jalapeño Pesto

Crushing fresh spices like chili and garlic together with salt brings out their flavors. You can't cheat by mixing the chili and garlic in a blender. This aromatic bomb will really lift the flavors of chicken and meat. It is also excellent with *Feijoada* in no time (page 128), or Refried Beans (page 140).

4 large, red chili peppers, preferably jalapeño (about 1.8 oz / 50 g)
4 garlic cloves (about 0.7 oz / 20 g)
1 tbsp coarse salt
1 oz (30 g) pine nuts
1 cup (50g) pecorino, or parmesan (grated)
²/₅ cup (100 ml) olive oil

Remove the seeds from the chili peppers. Peel the garlic cloves. Chop chili and garlic, and transfer to a mortar. Crush with salt. If your mortar isn't big enough, you can crush one half at a time. Transfer the garlic and chili to a different bowl. Crush the pine nuts coarsely, and save about a third of them for later. Add cheese and pine nuts (both the crushed, and the whole) into the chili blend. Add olive oil, a little bit at a time, until you achieve a creamy consistency.

Pomegranate & Walnut Salsa

Pomegranate seeds are one of the healthiest things you could eat. Walnuts are excellent with pomegranate, because they neutralize its acidity. Serve with chicken, salmon, or pork tenderloin instead of sauce, or as a little side dish.

1 large pomegranate (about 1.1 lbs / 500 g)
8.8 oz (250 g) walnuts
1 large yellow onion (about 7 oz / 200 g)
1 tbsp oil, i.e. corn oil
1 tsp salt
freshly ground black pepper

Cut the pomegranate in half. Use the handle of a wooden spoon to knock against the peel until the seeds fall out. Gather the seeds in a large bowl. Chop half of the walnuts pretty finely, and chop the remaining walnuts until they get a powder-like texture. One way to do that is to pulse them in a blender, remove half of the nuts, and keep mixing the remaining walnuts in the blender until they turn into a fine powder. Another option is to crush them in a mortar.

Roast the walnuts in a dry frying pan over medium heat. Make sure to shake them often to prevent them from burning. Begin by roasting the chopped walnuts, then the powdered ones. Chop the onion, and cook in neutral oil over medium heat until it turns transparent. Combine all the ingredients and taste to see if you need to add more salt.

Red Hummus

This hummus gets its flavor from ripened red pepper—the main ingredient in *ajvar* relish. This recipe requires a blender or a hand mixer. If you are using canned (already cooked) chickpeas, this hummus will only take a few minutes to prepare. Red hummus is excellent with everything: fish, chicken, or meat. You can store it in the fridge for several weeks in a jar with a tightly fitted lid.

1 ¾ oz (800 g) chickpeas, cooked
1 ⅓ cups *ajvar* relish, mild or regular
1 lemon, the juice
2 tbsp olive oil
1 tsp salt

Drain the chickpeas from the liquid. Combine the ingredients in a blender, or in a deep bowl if you are using a hand mixer. It may be more practical to mix the hummus directly in the glass jar that you are going to store it in.

Purple Hummus

Beets are underestimated. Healthy, good value, delicious, and beautiful. They give this hummus its gorgeous purple color and tasty flavor. I prefer to keep the cooking time short in the microwave to get a nice crunchy texture in my hummus, but keep in mind that that will require more arm strength if you are using a hand mixer.

1 ¾ lbs (800 g) chickpeas, cooked
17 oz (500 g) beets
1 tsp salt
2 tbsp olive oil
1 tsp water
1 lemon, the juice
2 tbsp tahini

Drain the chickpeas. Peel the beets, cut them into pieces, and heat in the microwave for 5–7 minutes at 500 watts together with salt, olive oil, and water. Test the consistency of the beets with a fork, and heat for longer if you want the consistency softer. Combine the beets with chickpeas, lemon juice, and tahini. Mix in a blender, or with a hand mixer, until you have a smooth paste. You can store the hummus in a glass jar and seal it with plastic wrap, or store the beets in a plastic container with a lid.

Carrot Hummus

Carrots turn this hummus absolutely golden yellow. Cumin gives it an irresistible aroma reminiscent of India. This is usually the favorite condiment among the guests at my table.

1 ¾ oz (800 g) chickpeas, cooked
4–5 carrots (about 1 lbs / 450 g)
2 tbsp olive oil
1 tsp sugar
1 tsp salt
1 lemon, the juice

3 tsp tahini
8 grilled garlic cloves with some of
    their own oil (page 160)
½ tsp cumin, ground
⅕–⅖ cup (10–20 g) chopped parsley

Drain the chickpeas. Peel the carrots if necessary. If the peel is very thin, it's enough just to scrub the carrots. Cut them into pieces, and put them with olive oil, sugar, and salt in a plastic bowl with a lid, or glass jar that you cover with plastic wrap. Heat in the microwave for 5 minutes at 500 watts. Mix all the ingredients, except for the parsley, in a blender/ food processor. You can also use a hand mixer, but then you'll need a very deep bowl, or you'll have the hummus flying all over the place. If you don't have grilled garlic cloves ready, you can press some garlic cloves into a skillet, and fry them with a tablespoon of oil over medium heat for 3 minutes for a fairly mild flavor. You can also use raw garlic, but only use 2–3 cloves if you decide to do so. Mix until the hummus turns into a smooth blend. Use a spatula to stir the parsley into the hummus.

Super Spicy Tamarind Paste

I recommend this flavor explosion to everyone. The paste is included in the Grilled Chicken Thigh Fillets with Spicy Tamarind Paste (page 40), but you can also use it as a condiment with chicken, pork tenderloin, and meat. It is great for flavoring stir-fried vegetables. One teaspoon provides plenty of tang. You can buy a jar of tamarind concentrate at an Asian food market, where it won't be too expensive. You can dilute the concentrate with a little bit of water, or stir some into a glass of orange juice for a very refreshing drink.

2 large roots of ginger (about 5.3 oz / 150 g)
2–4 tbsp tamarind concentrate
2 tsp cumin, ground
2 tsp black pepper, ground
2 tsp black pepper, ground
1 tbsp salt
2 tsp cardamom, ground
2 tsp coriander, ground

Peel and grate the cardamom. Combine the ingredients in the same jar that you are going to store the paste in. The recipe calls for 2 to 4 tablespoons, depending on the quality of the tamarind concentrate, which can vary widely in its strength and consistency. If you have a really thick concentrate, use less of it, but if it is more watery, you will need to use more. Taste, and add more if you want the paste more tart.

TIP FOR LUNCH BOX: Slice a piece of pork tenderloin thinly. Turn the slices in a teaspoon of tamarind paste and a teaspoon of rapeseed oil. Heat in the microwave for 2 minutes, and serve immediately with rice or bulgur.

Homemade Red Pesto

You can buy red pesto with sundried tomatoes at the grocery store, but the price per pound will be a lot higher than if you make it yourself. The homemade kind is a lot tastier too, and really simple to make. Sometimes, sundried tomatoes can be very dry, and other times they may be very moist and plump. Therefore, you should soak them in water for a few hours, and then squeeze out the liquid. If the tomatoes are very dry to begin with, keep in mind that they will double in weight after you soak them, while the soft tomatoes won't increase in weight as much. You can mix this pesto with freshly cooked pasta and a little bit of cream, and you'll have a delicious pasta dish in no time!

7 oz (200 g) sundried tomatoes (weigh after soaking)
5–6 garlic cloves
⅕ cup (50 ml) olive oil
2 tbsp linseed oil
2 tbsp balsamic vinegar
1 tsp salt
1 tbsp black pepper (whole)
2.1 oz (60 g) pine nuts
⅕ cup (10 g) parsley, chopped
1 ¾ cup (80 g) parmesan, grated

Cut the tomatoes into pieces or strips so that they are easier to chop in the blender. Peel the garlic cloves. Place the tomatoes, garlic, oil, vinegar, and salt in a blender. Mix until the tomatoes are finely blended. Crush the black pepper in a mortar. Crush the pine nuts coarsely in a mortar. Mix pepper, pine nuts, parsley, and parmesan. Season with more salt if necessary. You can add more water or oil if you want the consistency more fluid.

TIP: If you don't like the smell or flavor of garlic to be too strong, you can use grilled garlic cloves instead. Make sure to add a few extra cloves if you do so. Grilled garlic is a lot milder, and won't give you the same intense garlic breath.

Grilled Garlic

Grilled garlic is included in many recipes in this book. It's delicious with meat, chicken, vegetables, and it can really lift the flavors of a sauce, stir-fry, or stew when you are improvising a meal. In other words, it is always good to keep some grilled garlic on hand. Use a spoon to remove the garlic cloves and store them in a jar with olive oil. Shake them around so that they are entirely covered with oil. You can store them like this in the fridge for several weeks, and for months in the freezer. If you thaw the frozen garlic cloves for 10 minutes, you can just lift out as many as you need, and put the jar back into the freezer. The olive oil gets a delicious flavor from the garlic, so use it when you fry your vegetables.

4 x whole garlic
4 tbsp olive oil

Preheat the oven to 400 degrees. If the garlic has many loose layers of peel, rub them off with your hands. Cut off the top part of the garlic. Use a sharp, little knife so that you cut through each clove. Brush generously with olive oil. For best result, pack each garlic in aluminum foil, otherwise the surface of the garlic may get burnt, and spoil the flavor. Grill for 25 minutes.

Loosen the garlic cloves with a teaspoon, or with the tip of a knife. You can also serve an entire garlic per person, so that the guests can squeeze out their own cloves over their meal.

Anchovy Dressing

This dressing contains very little fat, but tastes very creamy. It can be stored in the fridge for several weeks if you keep it in a tightly sealed container.

½ lemon, the juice
10 anchovy fillets (0.7 oz / 20 g)
10 grilled garlic cloves, and a few tablespoons of their oil (page 158)
1 garlic clove
10 black peppercorns
1 tsp mustard
1 tsp capers
2 eggs
1 tbsp water

Use a hand mixer to combine all the ingredients, except for the eggs and water. Crack the eggs into a plastic container with a tightly fitted lid, and add the water. Heat the eggs and water in the microwave for 30 seconds at 500 watts. The eggs should be lightly cooked—the whites will have coagulated, but not the yolks (you may need to cook them for an additional 10–20 seconds). Mix the eggs with the remaining ingredients.

Tapenade

There are about as many different recipes for tapenade as there are chefs around the Mediterranean. This is my refreshing variation. It is excellent with fish, chicken and boiled meat. Tapenade on a piece of bread is a very nice appetizer, but can also be included in a main course.

½ lemon
1 garlic clove
10 anchovy fillets (about 0.7 oz / 20 g)
1 tbsp capers
⅘ cup (about 60 g) black olives, pitted
2–3 tbsp olive oil
freshly ground black pepper

Grate the lemon peel finely, but without any of the white part. Squeeze the lemon and set the fresh juice aside for now. Peel and slice the garlic clove thinly. Chop lemon peel, garlic, anchovies, capers, and olives. If you want, you can combine everything in a food processor or blender, but I prefer it when you can tell different ingredients apart to when it's a smooth paste. Stir the olive oil into the mix, and season with lemon juice and black pepper.

TIP: Add a can of tuna to a batch of tapenade. Chop up two boiled eggs, and gently stir them into the tapenade. Now, you have a delicious tuna salad that tastes good on a sandwich, or in a complete meal when combined with rice or pasta.

Foods for Endurance Training

Here, we teach you what you need to know when planning your diet for the best possible results during endurance training.

Most endurance-training athletes make the same mistake. They don't eat enough to sustain their energy needs. Mostly, this happens out of fear of gaining weight, and as a consequence they actually lower their performance ability. If you don't eat enough to cover your energy needs, you will automatically lower your ability to perform optimally. The trick is to increase your energy needs with foods that are nutritionally dense, and packed with vitamins, minerals, and antioxidants. By putting together your own meals according to the principles presented in this book—combining a source of protein, carbohydrates, vegetable side, and a flavor addition—it becomes very easy. Let us use the Pomegranate & Walnut Salsa (page 154) as an example. It provides you with plenty of vitamins, antioxidants, and healthy fats from the walnuts. Tomato & Mango Salsa (page 109), and Sesame Fried Vegetables (page 86) are other examples.

Endurance-training athletes that work out intensely and often usually have an increased need for iron and calcium, which can easily be fulfilled through their diet. To maximize iron absorption, try to combine iron-rich dishes with flavor additions or vegetables that are packed with vitamin C, which boosts the body's ability to absorb the iron. As an example, it would be a good idea to combine a meat dish with Spinach salad with almonds and orange dressing, on page 104. You can also make sure to cook your food in a cast iron pot/pan.

You Need Plenty of Protein

Endurance athletes are, contrary to what many people believe, the type of athletes that have the highest protein need. That's because they tend to empty their carbohydrate energy depot during their workout, and once the body uses up carbohydrates, it will start using proteins for energy. With endurance athletes, they also tend to lose some of the proteins through urination. Just like with any other types of athletes, the protein is necessary for the post-workout reparation and maintenance of muscles. If you are in endurance training, you should aim at consuming about 0.04–0.07 oz (1.2–2 grams) of protein per 2.2 pounds (1 kilogram) per day. If you are only working out at a low exercise level, about 1 hour a week, this rule does not apply. If you belong to the elite level of exercise enthusiasts with several workouts scheduled into your week, including long distance sessions and interval training each week, you should aim for the higher value. Even when you have a higher protein need, you can still fulfill that requirement through your diet. Preferably, choose meals where you get extra protein in addition to the protein source—meat, fish, and poultry. Good protein-rich accompaniments: Baltic Herring Gratin with Feta (page 66), Chickpea Stew from North Africa (page 100), and Hash with Chickpeas & Chicken (page 42). Also pick side dishes that are protein-rich, such as the various Hummus variations on pages 156–157, or the Tahini Pesto on page 150. It doesn't hurt if you also combine your meal with any of the protein-rich vegetables options, such as Pink Coleslaw (page 102) or Spinach Salad with Almonds and Orange Dressing (page 106).

Fats Help You Save Carbohydrates

Endurance athletes tend to avoid fat like it is the plague because they want to avoid anything that will make them gain weight, and give them extra weight to carry around. There is logic behind that reasoning: It takes more energy to move a heavy body, and as an endurance-training athlete it usually pays off to be fairly light in weight. However, dramatically decreasing your fat intake is never a good idea. Fat is a very important energy source, and helps you save your carbohydrates during your exercise sessions so that you can work out intensely for longer. When you are using up many calories per day, a moderate fat intake is important if you want to keep your serving sizes somewhat normal. The lower your fat intake, the more food you will need to eat to cover your energy need without feeling like your tummy has four corners after each meal.

How much fat should you consume? Well, different types of endurance athletes require different quantities of fat. If you know that you burn fat really quickly, and therefore easily lose weight, your daily energy intake should consist of about 25–30% fat. If your metabolism isn't quite as effective, or if you aren't working out as hard, you should aim for 20% instead. How you exercise matters. If your endurance training is always at a low/medium intensity level, you can keep your fat intake a little bit higher than if you also mix it up with interval training, and other high-intensity workouts. High-intensity training requires carbohydrates, while low- and medium-intensity workouts are best fueled with a mix of carbohydrates and fats.

No matter what fat intake you decide to aim for, it is always a good idea to be picky about what kind of fats you are consuming. Preferably eat fish at least three times a week, because fish contains plenty of healthy omega-3 fatty acids. Omega-3's may improve the transportation of oxygen and nutrients to the muscles and other tissues by reducing blood viscosity, improving oxygen-dependent digestion, reducing inflammation, and shortening the recovery process after exercise. If you are in endurance training, you will reap huge benefits from eating a lot of fish. Also vary the types of fish that you consume. Farm-raised fish are usually cheaper, but unfortunately they tend to contain high levels of pollutants and heavy metals. Limit your consumption of farm-raised fish to once a week or try to buy wild-caught fish. Children, and women who are trying to get pregnant, are pregnant, or are breast-feeding should only eat such fish two to three times a year. This is also true for fatty prey fish from other waters, such as fresh tuna fish, skate, swordfish, Atlantic halibut, and shark. Canned tuna is usually of a different type, and can be eaten freely. You can consume salmon, (including farm-raised), and other types of fish from the Arctic Ocean several times a week.

Another way to make sure that you get enough fatty acids, and a good balance between saturated and polyunsaturated fat, is to choose lean meat that you can combine with flavor additions and provide you with healthy polyunsaturated fat, i.e. Homemade Red Pesto, on page 159, or Tahini Pesto, on page 150.

Maximize Your Carbohydrate Intake

Endurance athletes have developed their ability to use fats as fuel, which saves their carbohydrates. The more fit you are, the higher intensity you can maintain and still burn a high amount of fat. But you still need carbohydrates to maintain your intensity, and after two hours of exercising, your carbohydrate fuel storage will be empty. Then, you will need to lower your speed significantly, or stop the workout. To be able to maintain the intensity when you exercise, you need to make sure that you are well-stocked with carbohydrates. A low-carbohydrate diet is not beneficial for the endurance athlete, as it won't yield optimal workout results.

When you are primarily in endurance training, the majority of your carbohydrate intake should consist of medium-fast carbohydrates. If you eat primarily slow carbohydrates, you won't store enough carbohydrates in the muscles, as this process requires a certain amount of insulin in order for the storage deposits to be effective. In addition, a diet that primarily contains low carbohydrates is very filling, which makes it difficult to eat enough. To avoid having to eat gigantic portions you should aim for a medium-high GI value.

When Should You Eat?

You can manage low-intensity endurance training on an empty stomach, as long as you don't do it for long periods at a time. During the night, when the body is fasting, your carbohydrate storage in the muscles will run low. Then the body will need to use a high amount of fat to produce energy, which makes it impossible to perform high-intensity training. Long distance training, such as intense speed and interval training should only be performed after you've had time to refill the body's carbohydrate depots through at least one meal that day, but preferably more than that.

If you eat two hours before your workout, your meal should primarily contain carbohydrates with a low GI, so that your blood sugar doesn't drop too low while working out. It will also improve the fat burning process during the exercise session, which will save your carbohydrate depots.

During workout sessions that are 90 minutes or longer, you may need to refill your carbohydrate intake and drink more fluids. Make sure that those are fast-acting carbohydrates so that they have time to be absorbed by your bloodstream and prove effective during the physical exercise. Best is if you consume carbohydrates in liquid form, i.e. a sports drink. However, you don't need to spend money on expensive energy drinks. You can make your own at home. At www.matforresultat. se you can learn how to make your own energy drinks, recovery drinks, and energy bars. It is simple, inexpensive, and won't contain any food dyes, preservatives, stabilizers, or any other additives that often can be found in the store-bought kinds.

If more than one hour passes between your last workout and your next meal, you should eat or drink at least a little snack that contains fast-acting carbohydrates and proteins right after your workout. This is to jump start the recovery process, and to facilitate the carbohydrate storage in the muscles. Because your body requires a lot of liquid after a long and intense workout, it is a good idea to have a mini snack in the shape of a recovery drink that you can make at home. If you eat a regular meal within an hour of your workout, it should contain some fast carbohydrates so that you facilitate maximal storage in your carbohydrate depots.

Food for Weight Training

This chapter teaches you what to eat to increase, or maintain, the muscle mass that you have gained through weight training. The tips here are great for anyone who trains for any other strength sports of the anaerobic or explosive nature.

Most people in weight training that aim to build muscle mass are relying too heavily on proteins. Sure, adequate quantities of protein are very important to yield positive results in your weight training, but carbohydrates are just as important to stimulate the best possible development of the muscle mass.

Many people that perform weight-training aim to build muscle mass and simultaneously decrease their body fat. Unfortunately, this is seldom possible. To build your muscles, you need excess energy storage, and less body fat contributes to a lower energy source. A diet that maximizes the fat burning process and leads to weight loss is different than a diet that aims to build muscle. To unite these two goals, it is wise to switch between weeks and months of extra heavy and intense workouts combined with a diet that stimulates maximal muscle growth, and weeks of less intense workouts combined with a slightly lower calorie intake and a diet that maximizes the fat burning process. That strategy matches well with the principle of periodization: for successful training, and to prevent injuries or to avoid overworking the muscles, high intensity heavy exercise periods should always be followed with intervals of lighter, less intense training. We will go over the diet strategies for the muscle building periods in this chapter, and you will learn about the diet strategies for the fat burning intervals in the chapter about foods for muscle definition, on page 177.

Protein to Build Muscle

An adequate intake of protein is a given if you want to increase your muscle mass. The protein is required to repair the microscopic injuries that occur in the muscles during exercise, to build more muscle mass, and, in smaller amounts, to use as energy during the workout.

The more muscle mass you have, the more protein your body will require because a bigger muscle mass requires more protein for reparation and maintenance. Count on at least 1.2–2 grams of protein per 2.2 pounds of bodyweight per day. The lower value is for people who are hobby athletes, and don't have any major muscle building ambitions. The higher value is primarily for people who are exercising on an elite level, or if they combine their weight training with a lot of endurance training. Contrary to what many people believe, endurance training requires a lot more protein than workouts intended to increase your muscle mass, partially because more protein is required to sustain endurance training, and people who are in endurance training tend to lose a lot of protein through urination.

It is wise to err on the side of consuming less protein than eating too much of it. When the body has taken care of the amino acids it needs, the remaining amino acids are converted into ammonia. Ammonia is toxic to the body, but is converted into urea by enzymes in the liver, and excreted during urination. The more protein you consume, the more ammonia is produced, which means that the body has to work harder to detoxify.

Considering that most people that exercise are consciously making healthy choices to eat pure and non-toxic food, it is rather counterproductive to take supplements that force the body to work harder to detoxify. In addition, you will smell like ammonia, especially when you sweat, and that is rather unpleasant. The remaining residue from the amino acid transformation will mainly be stored as fat, which is something nobody wants if they are a workout enthusiast.

What does it mean to meet your energy need? We've already established that you should consume about 1.2–2 grams of protein per 2.2 pounds (1 kg) of body weight per day. If you weigh 176 pounds (80 kg), your body requires between 96 and 160 grams of protein per day. If you wish to increase your muscle mass by 11 lbs (5 kg), you need to meet that protein requirement, about 102–170 grams of protein per day. You need to use your common sense here. You can't just stuff yourself with proteins and hope that your muscles will grow. You have to train intensely and use enough weights to stimulate such muscle growth. That requires you to be realistic about how much you can increase your muscle mass within a certain time limit. If you have been working out for a long time, you've probably noticed that it takes a lot of work just to increase the muscle mass by 3.5–7 (1–2 hg) ounces. In addition, you need to have enough energy and time to work out as often, and as hard, as is required to achieve the desired muscle mass. It isn't just about the time you spend at the gym: the harder you work out, the more time your body needs to recover, and it will require more sleep and other recovery processes. An increased intake of protein helps, but it doesn't solve the entire muscle building equation on its own.

Most people that perform weight/strength training are well aware of the increased protein need. However, they also tend to believe that the more proteins they consume, the better. It leads them to buy expensive protein supplements that are unnecessary. It is easy to cover your protein need through your diet if you eat a variety of foods at adequate serving sizes. Keep in mind that it isn't just the typical protein sources such as meat, fish, poultry, and egg that provide you with proteins. Dairy products such as milk, yogurt, and cheese have a high protein content, as do nuts, seeds, and legumes. Baltic Herring Gratin (page 66) is a great example of a dish that has maximized is protein content that way. Homemade hummus, like the three variations on pages 156–157, provide your main dish with an addition of proteins. Dishes such as Chickpea Stew from North Africa (page (100) and *Feijoada* (page 128) can easily be adjusted to maximize their protein content. The Spinach Salad with Almonds and Orange Dressing (page 106) is a vegetable dish with very high protein content thanks to the yogurt and almonds. You can always increase your protein intake by drinking a glass of milk with your meal.

There are several reasons why you should fulfill your daily protein need through your diet, rather than through supplements. Many people believe that dietary supplements have a more concentrated source of amino acids per serving. A piece of meat that weighs about 1 ounce (30 g) contains about 7000 milligrams amino acids, while a typical protein supplement contains between 500 to 1000 milligrams amino acids per serving. Many of the supplements contain amino acids that the body is unable to recognize, and is therefore unable to absorb. Therefore, the number of amino acids promised on the packaging may differ from the actual number that the body is able to process. Other reasons to choose your diet as your source of protein are that it is more environmentally friendly, tastier, and you won't consume as many artificial flavors, dyes, thickeners, and preservatives. Protein is fairly expensive, so from an economic standpoint this is another reason to eat it in moderation.

Fat—An Important Source of Energy

When your exercise goal is to increase muscle mass, your energy intake should be slightly higher than your exact need. If you only eat enough to repair the body after a workout, you will maintain the muscles you already have, but you won't be able to build any additional muscles. If your workouts are intense for the purpose of muscle building, you will need to consume enough energy to sustain that. To avoid eating to the point where you feel like your stomach is about to burst, your energy consumption should consist of energy-rich foods; each gram of fat provides 50% more energy than 1 gram of protein or carbohydrates. In addition, fat is an important flavor component, and it will make you feel full faster, and for longer.

However, you want to keep your fat intake at a moderate level. Most people who do weight/strength training are striving to look more defined, which means that they want to keep their subcutaneous fat layer low. The trick is to keep your fat intake at a level where you get enough energy without too much effort, but don't consume so much that you gain more body fat. You will need to experiment until you find what works for you, because it is an individual matter. If you are tall and slim, and have to fight hard to gain even the slightest ounce of weight, you will need to keep your fat intake high, about 30% of your total energy consumption. The same rule applies if you do a lot of endurance training in addition to strength training. On the contrary, if you easily gain weight you can lower your fat intake to around 20%. Make sure to lower the fat intake slowly and gradually. If you don't consume enough fat, you will feel hungry instead and crave foods that are unhealthy. Never lower your fat intake to below 20%, unless your doctor advises it. When you exercise hard, your body requires more energy, but also more vitamins. Without a sufficient amount of fat in your diet, your body will be unable to absorb the fat-soluble vitamins: A, D, E, and K. A low fat intake also means that you will need to eat more to cover your energy need and many people can't consume quantities that are large enough to cover that need, which may lead to malnutrition and can disturb the body's hormone production in the long run.

No matter what level of fat intake you are aiming for, it is important that you make sure to consume enough healthy fats. You can do this by consuming fish (especially fish with a high fat content) a few times a week, and by adding nuts, seeds, avocado, and olives to your diet. Niclas teaches you how in the recipe section. The Berry Bulgur on page 134 is a great example of how you can complement a carbohydrate source with nuts to add healthy fats. Flavor additions such as Tahini Pesto (page 150) and Tahini Mayo (page 148) provide you with healthy fats, as does the Tapenade on page 163.

The Significance of Carbohydrates to Build Muscle Mass

It is important to eat enough carbohydrates to have enough energy to be able to exercise intensely, while making it possible for the body to save the protein rather than using it up as energy. A deficient carbohydrate intake will release the hormones cortisol and glucogan, which break down muscle mass. By keeping the glycemic index in your diet under control, you can plan your diet to achieve maximal muscle building effect. You have probably heard that insulin, the hormone that is released in the body when we eat carbohydrates to facilitate the transportation of blood sugar to the muscles and the liver, increases body fat. However, the hormone also stimulates muscle growth. The trick is to maximize the muscle building effect without accumulating too much fat. You can't entirely avoid increased fat storage during the muscle building periods, but by exercising regularly at an intense level, you will develop good insulin sensitivity. If you eat several small meals a day, rather than a few large ones, your body's fat storage will be minimal, while you will achieve a rapid increase in muscle growth. You will get rid of any extra fat during the definition periods that should come after about a month of the building periods, which should last about a month as well.

Fast carbohydrates—carbs with a high GI value—stimulate the highest insulin secretion, and therefore they facilitate a fast muscle building effect. However, you want to avoid a rebound effect. That's when a quick and powerful rise in the blood sugar levels leads to insulin release, which causes the blood sugar levels to drop shortly after the meal to levels below what they were prior to the meal. You want to avoid having your blood glucose levels drop too low during your workout. To prevent this, you also need to eat medium-fast carbohydrates to steadily maintain your blood sugar levels over a longer time period. A good rule of thumb is to consume 50% fast carbohydrates, with a GI that exceeds 90, and 50% medium-fast carbohydrates, with a GI value between 60 and 90. What does this mean in practice? Most dishes in this book have a low or medium GI value, but there are a few dishes with a high GI. You also always have the option to combine a dish with a medium-level GI with a carbohydrate source with a high GI, such as white, polished rice, or a slice of white bread. You can also choose a high GI value drink with your meal, or eat something sweet after your meal.

What about slow carbohydrates then? Sure you can eat them, even during the build-up periods, but focus mostly on medium-fast and fast carbohydrates. Then, you will replace the quick carbohydrates with slow carbohydrates during the definition periods.

When Should You Eat?

Avoid strength training on an empty stomach. Strength training is the type of anaerobic exercise where the body uses carbohydrates, not fat, to produce energy. If you don't have enough carbohydrates in your body's energy depots, you won't have the energy to exercise as hard, and your body will be forced to break down muscle mass to use protein as an emergency energy source. You should eat about five small meals a day to achieve maximal effect and to avoid negative effects from the high GI carbohydrates during the build-up weeks. If you work out during your lunch-break, you can use the energy source consumed during your breakfast and morning snack. If you exercise after work, you will also have had lunch and an afternoon snack, so your body will have enough carbohydrates to draw its energy from by that point.

If there is more than an hour between your completed workout and your next meal, you should at least make sure to eat a snack directly after exercising that consists of fast carbohydrates and some proteins. It could be a drinking yogurt, a homemade smoothie sweetened with a little bit of sugar or honey (or sweet berries) to provide quick carbs, a sandwich with white bread, or something similar. If you are going to eat a proper meal within an hour of your completed workout, you don't need to eat a snack directly after exercising.

Foods For Muscle Definition

The concept of defining or toning your muscles within the world of body building means that you are aiming to decrease body fat, while maintaining as much muscle mass as possible so that the muscles look clearly defined. This chapter teaches you what to eat to succeed with your high definition training.

One of the conditions for successful high definition results without any of the negative health effects is to build up the muscle mass to a moderate level, and to start when your body fat is at a level where you don't need to get rid of much. You won't need as much muscle mass as a body builder, but you should at least have increased a few pounds in muscle mass since you began your fitness routine. You shouldn't aim for high definition training if you are already very skinny. If you don't have any body fat to get rid of, but train to get more defined, you'll only lose muscle mass, slow down your metabolism, risk hormonal imbalance, and negatively affect the immune system. Women, especially, risk developing osteoporosis if their body fat percentage is too low for an extended period of time.

    Most people who spend time at the gym are looking to increase their muscle mass, while simultaneously decreasing their body fat. This is really only possible when you are new to exercising and are able to increase your muscle mass relatively quickly (which increases your metabolism), while the workout increases your calorie burn. Once your body is used to exercising, it will take longer to build muscle. It requires extra energy and a diet that facilitates the muscle building process, and optimization of the fat burning process requires a diet that has a low GI and, possibly, a lower calorie intake. To achieve the ideal shape, you will benefit from switching between muscle building periods—see the chapter about foods for strength training on page 169—with intervals of high definition workouts. A muscle definition period should last about 4 weeks. It can be longer, but if you are working out hard, you shouldn't exercise to define muscles for too long because you will begin to break down your muscle mass instead. In turn, your immune system and your hormone levels will be negatively affected. Most people who exercise regularly are unable to stay healthy with a very low body fat percentage.

Protein To Maintain Muscle Mass

To maintain your muscle mass, it is important that you get enough protein. Even if you lower your entire calorie intake, you should be sure to maintain the same protein intake, about 0.04–0.07 oz (1.2–2 grams) per 2.2 pounds (1 kilogram) of body weight per day. Aim for the lower number if you only do strength training, but for the higher amount if you are also in endurance training. The table below gives you an idea of this concept.

Your Weight	Your Daily Protein Requirement
132 lbs (60 kg)	72–120 grams
143 lbs (65 kg)	78–130 grams
154 lbs (70 kg)	84–140 grams
165 lbs (75 kg)	90–150 grams
176 lbs (80 kg)	96–160 grams
187 lbs (85 kg)	102–170 grams

If you weigh 176 pounds (80 kg), you shouldn't exceed 160 grams of protein a day, which is what a steak that weighs 12.5 ounces (350 g) provides. You can easily consume that divided over two meals (and then we're not even counting the protein you ate at breakfast, and snack time). It is more important that you consume 1.2–2 grams of protein per 2.2 pounds (1 kg) of body weight per day, than worrying about what percentage of your daily diet consists of protein.

A Little Less Fat, But Only A Little

The most common mistake that exercise enthusiasts make is that when they aim to lose weight, they lower their fat intake to a minimum. It may seem logical, but in practice this actually slows down the metabolism and the fat burning process, which makes it more difficult for the body to absorb fat-soluble vitamins. When we eat less fat, we also tend to feel hungry even after a meal, which leads us to snack more in-between meals. The amount of fat needed to achieve maximal fat burning, while feeling satisfied, is an individual matter. Some people can keep their fat intake at up to 30% of their daily calorie consumption, while other people need to keep their fat consumption lower to succeed with their muscle definition goal. We advise that you never lower your fat intake below 20% of your daily caloric intake. More important is to watch what kind of fats you are consuming. Try to avoid hydrogenated fats and trans fats as much as possible.

How? Eat home cooked meals made with high quality produce, rather than semi-processed, or processed foods. Also, be sure to keep a good balance between saturated, unsaturated, and polyunsaturated fats, and to consume enough healthy omega-3 fatty acids. In practice, this means that you should eat mainly lean animal source protein, such as chicken fillet, turkey, lamb, and veal. The majority of your fat intake should come from nuts, seeds, avocado, fatty fish, and healthy oils. Speedy Salmon with Coconut & Jalapeño (page 62), and Octopus with Ginger & Garlic (page 48) are excellent examples of how you increase your omega-3 consumption. Flavor additions such as Homemade Red Pesto (page 159) and Tahini Pesto (page 150) are also packed with healthy fats.

Less Carbohydrates, More Slow Carbs

To achieve the best possible results when trying to gain more muscle definition, about half of the produce you eat should have a low GI value, while the other half should have a medium GI value. Slow carbohydrates fill you up faster and keep you satisfied longer, while optimizing the fat burning process. The medium-fast ones are needed to effectively store carbohydrates in the muscles, and to stimulate enough insulin production to maintain muscle mass. If you mostly eat produce with a low GI you may lose weight quicker, but you are also likely to lose some of the muscle mass that you have worked so hard to build up.

It may sound complicated to eat one half slow and one half fast carbohydrates, but there is nothing strange about it. The majority of traditional carbs, such as pasta and rice, belong to the group of medium release carbohydrates, while vegetables provide slow release carbohydrates. Also keep in mind that the flavor additions and drinks with meals usually add carbohydrates as well. You don't need to split the carbohydrates exactly down to the gram, 50/50, when it comes to slow and medium release carbs—each individual has their own insulin sensitivity and exercise intensity level. You will discover what works best for you after a few weeks of experimentation.

Nowadays, many low-carb diets receive plenty of media attention, but we want to stress that you should never lower your carbohydrate intake too low. To achieve optimal muscle definition results, you need the energy to work out hard enough to maintain your muscle mass and, ideally, also to include some type of fat burning workout into your exercise regimen. A very low carbohydrate intake will leave you feeling depleted, break down muscle mass, and lower the fat burning process in the body. First and foremost, you should adjust the type of carbohydrates that you eat. If you want to lower your total carbohydrate intake, you should do it in very small steps. Without sufficient energy, your muscles won't become more defined.

Don't Forget The Flavor Additions

A common strategy among people who are looking to gain more definition is to eat various selected food items, instead of actual meals. A classic example: chicken fillet, a pile of rice, and a tomato. They do it to avoid unnecessary calories, but flavor additions don't have to mean unnecessary calories. The flavor additions that Niclas presents in this book contain many vitamins, minerals, antioxidants, and other healthy additions. Homemade Red Pesto (page 159) is packed with healthy fats and calcium, and the garlic oils contain the active organosulfur compound allicin, which has antibacterial properties for preventing cardiovascular diseases. Coconut Pesto with Green Chili (page 152) helps speed up your metabolism thanks to the chili, while there's less risk of coconut fat becoming stuck in fat cells, compared to other types of fat. Likewise, Red Jalapeño Pesto (page 152) also speeds up the metabolism. Pomegranate & Walnut Salsa (page 154) is an antioxidant boost that also contains healthy fats and fibers.

Foods that Increase Fat Burning

When the food you eat is converted into energy in the body, some of the calories in the meal are used to facilitate this process. Metabolism also generates heat, referred to as thermogenesis. About 10 percent of the calories you eat are used up during this process. If your energy consumption is somewhere between 2000 and 5000 calories a day, we are talking about 200 to 500 calories per day. You can increase thermogenesis through certain food choices. Protein increases the energy consumption by 30 percent, carbohydrates by five percent, and fat by one percent. It is important to keep a relatively high protein consumption during your muscle definition periods to maintain muscle mass, but also to speed up your metabolism.

However, that is not all. There are also some spices that increase thermogenesis, so incorporating them into your cooking in simple and delicious ways will increase the fat burning process. Garlic, chili, cayenne pepper, mustard, horseradish, ginger, curry, cardamom, and cinnamon are good examples of thermogenic spices. Quick Cured Salmon with Lime and Ginger (page 60) and Fish Stew from Lamu (page 54) are two excellent examples of meals that stimulate fat burning. Green tea also has a thermogenic effect on the body.

and you can happily drink it with your meal. Try to include some sort of thermogenic spice into each meal. Cinnamon is delicious with porridge or yogurt, cardamom tastes great in homemade milk drinks, and cottage cheese pairs well with fruit salad or a berry blend.

Thermogenic spices and foods are not miracle cures. You won't experience fat melting off your body just because you season your meal with ginger or jalapeño. The effect can be compared to a power walk in the morning before breakfast. You won't burn more calories, but the calories you burn come from fat rather than carbohydrates (like when you exercise right after a meal rather than on an empty stomach). Best-case scenario, we are only talking about a few grams. But when you are looking to gain muscle definition, that's exactly what you want. If you are already toned you don't really have excess fat, but you want more chiseled details in your muscle tone.

When Should You Eat?

To feel energized, and to keep your fat burning ratio at maximum, it is important that you eat several small meals a day, rather than a few large ones. Five meals a day is ideal. If your workouts are at a low intensity on the fat burning front, such as walking, you can perform them before breakfast. However, you should at least have had breakfast, and preferably something more, before you begin your strength training session. Strength training usually requires well-filled carbohydrate depots. If you exercise after work you may have to eat your evening meal really late. Have you ever heard that everything you eat after a certain hour in the evening will be stored as fat? Well, you can relax—it is just a myth. On the other hand, a lot of people have trouble sleeping if they consume a large meal right before they go to bed. Instead, you can make sure to eat a larger afternoon snack, so that your evening meal can be smaller.

Foods For Weight Loss

This chapter is for anyone who is carrying around a few extra pounds, and wishes to lose this weight. Perhaps you move around a lot every day, but only exercise once or twice a week, or every once in a while on an irregular basis. The diet strategies in this chapter are great for anyone who just started an exercise routine and wishes to drop a few pounds, but doesn't work out often or at an intense level.

The basic principle behind losing weight is simple: You have to consume fewer calories than you burn. Unfortunately, a lot of people think this means that the less you eat, the better. That is a myth. If your energy consumption is too low, your metabolism will slow down and it will become harder to lose weight and burn fat. Instead, you become tired, weak, and deprived of energy to exercise. If you work out anyway, you will be tired from the lack of energy rather than from the workout. You won't have the energy to exercise hard enough to achieve results, and chances are your muscle mass will break down and your metabolism will slow down. A very low caloric intake also leads to a sweet tooth and hunger attacks, which contribute to more snacking in between meals and eating portions that are way too large during lunch and dinner. You may be able to resist these urges during your first or second week while you are still highly motivated, but sooner or later most people give up and return to their previous eating habits—the ones that caused the extra pounds in the first place.

For successful weight loss, you need to lower your caloric intake just a notch, but not too much. Begin by decreasing—not cutting out—your less healthy eating habits. Eat less of your typical junk food like candy, cookies, chips, and beer. Doing this alone will save you countless calories, and achieve weight loss to some extent.

The Art of Feeling Full While Eating Less

Most likely, you will need to eat slightly smaller portions, and make some changes to your diet, in order to succeed with your desired weight loss. But to achieve weight loss that is sustainable, you also need to eat in a way that makes you feel satisfied. For starters, it is wise to keep a regular eating schedule, at least three but preferably five meals a day: breakfast, lunch, dinner, and one or two snacks. This will not only keep you feeling full and satisfied, but you will also feel more energized the entire day thanks to more stable blood sugar levels.

It is important to eat balanced meals that provide you with enough protein, fats, and carbohydrates. It also matters what type of fats and carbohydrates you choose, which you can read more about in the next few pages. The entire meal experience will have an impact on your overall mood and satisfaction. When you are able to sit down and eat your food in a serene environment, you will take your time and chew each bite more thoroughly—giving your body time to send signals to your brain when it is full. Compare that to when you devour a diet shake: it takes less than a minute, and you need to consciously stop yourself from eating more until your body signals that it is full. When we chew our food properly, it facilitates our metabolism. Several studies have proven that we feel more satisfied after a warm meal, which is a good reason to eat warm meals for breakfast, lunch, and dinner. By preparing meal boxes while preparing your dinner, you will always have access to a healthy alternative instead of unhealthy fast food. It will save you money and positively affect your shape, in addition to being a better choice for the environment.

Protein—Dare To Try New Sources

Protein is important to feel satisfied, and healthy people have no problems with high protein consumption. However, protein sources such as meat and fish are relatively expensive, and meat production has a higher environmental impact than vegetable source proteins such as beans, lentils, and chickpeas. To care for mother Earth, it is wise to choose some vegetable source proteins in place of meat and meat produce. Notice that we are not talking about an all-or-nothing approach here. You can achieve the desired effect by eating more fish, and protein-rich vegetables. What does that mean? Well, the following are examples of how you can approach this idea:

- Eat fish two to three times a week, and a vegetarian protein source one to two times a week.
- Decrease your meat portions so that they are about the size of a deck of cards, and allow yourself to enjoy protein-rich flavor additions such as the Hummus variations (pages 156–157) or Homemade Red Pesto (page 159). It will make the meal more delicious, beautiful, and packed with vitamins, minerals, and antioxidants.

- Combine meat with vegetable source proteins in the same meal, like in Hash with Chickpeas & Chicken on page 42.
- Use the protein portion of your meal as an addition, instead of the main component. When you want to lose weight, but don't exercise intensely several days a week, your protein need is only about 0.8 grams per 2.2 pounds (1 kg) of body weight per day. Even if you eat more protein to increase your thermogenesis and to feel full (see page 180), let's say 1.2–2 grams of protein per 2.2 pounds (1 kg) of body weight per day, you will easily cover your need by using the protein source as an addition. Complete your meal and protein requirements with protein-rich flavor additions, or vegetable and carbohydrate dishes that contain a lot of protein.

The Right Fat for Weight Loss

From a satisfaction perspective, each meal should have a good balance of protein, carbohydrates, and fats. Several of the current trendy diets, such as LCHF and ISO, are on the right track when they suggest a higher fat intake than is traditionally recommended for weight loss. Exactly how much fat to consume, and how to distribute it over different types of fat, is still an open-ended question. However, it is clear that fat has an important impact on how long we feel satisfied and how the food tastes. A diet that is too low in fat will slow down the metabolism. Between 20 to 30 percent of your daily total calories should come from fat, but experiment to see what works best for you. Some people do better on a diet with a higher fat content, while others feel better and lose weight more easily when they decrease their fat consumption slightly. The following advice gives you pointers on how to keep your fat intake at a moderate level, and simultaneously achieve a good balance between different fat sources:

- Keep eating meat, but rethink your serving sizes. A proper portion should be about the size of a deck of cards for optimal weight loss. This is after you have cut away non-edible pieces, such as bones, from the piece of meat.
- Eat fish two to three times a week, and vary between lean and fatty kinds.
- Be inspired by the use of meat in the healthy Mediterranean diet. Use meat to complement the meal, rather than being the main component. Instead, complement the meal with flavor additions that are rich in protein or fat, depending on your need. Try drizzling some Rapeseed Oil with Fresh Turmeric (page 150) over grilled root vegetables, fish, or chicken. Tapenade (page 163) is another flavor addition that contributes both protein and healthy fats to the meal.

Keep The Carbs in Check

You won't get fat just by eating carbohydrates. However, you will gain weight if you eat too many carbs, which is the same as when you eat too much protein, excessive fat, or if you eat mostly quick-release carbohydrates. Today, many people who are overweight have gotten that way because they eat too many carbs, and because the majority of these are fast carbohydrates from refined, nutritionally poor produce. This doesn't mean that all carbohydrates are dangerous. Instead, you should make sure that your carbohydrate intake consists mostly of slow carbs, and avoid eating massive portions of the carb dishes. What does this mean in practice?

- Eat more vegetables, root vegetables, fruits, and berries. In Sweden, we eat a meager 250 grams/day of fruit and vegetables on average, even though the recommended value is 500 grams/day. In other words, we need to double our intake! Most vegetables, root vegetables, fruits, and berries contain slow carbohydrates. You may disagree because you read somewhere that carrots have a high GI value. However, carrots, other root vegetables, and fruits are good examples of why you shouldn't stare yourself blind at the GI of produce. Instead, use your common sense. The GI value is based on 50 grams of usable carbs in food. If you focus solely on that value, carrots have a high GI. However, to reach 50 grams of usable carbs in carrots, you would need to consume about 1.8 pounds (800 g) of carrots! A regular carrot serving is about the size of a large carrot, 2.8–3.5 ounces (80–100 g). Here, the GI value is actually between 20 and 50, depending on if you eat the carrot cooked or raw—a low GI in either case. It is the same with most root vegetables and fruits that are considered to have a high GI.
- Vegetables, root vegetables, fruits, and berries provide a whole lot of fiber that keep you feeling fuller longer, and are packed with vitamins, antioxidants, and other important nutrients that help cover your daily nutritional needs without any added supplements—which also saves you money in the long run. Choose organic and locally farmed vegetables and fruits whenever possible.
- Eat smaller servings of flour products, such as pasta and bread. Choose whole grain whenever possible.
- Mix the pasta, rice, or the carbohydrate food of your choice with vegetables to increase the vegetable serving, but also to decrease the serving of flour and grain foods. Try the Berry Bulgur on page 134. If you want to lower the GI more, you can add fewer raisins.

- Try different carb sources, such as bulgur and wheat berries, and eat less processed carbohydrate foods, such as polished rice, quick noodles, and similar carbs.
- Choose unsweetened, or lightly sweetened cereal, müsli, jams, and other food products that otherwise may contain a lot of sugar.
- Watch out for invisible sugar. If you buy a latte at a café it may be sweetened, especially with flavor syrup, which provides you with a large dose of fast carbohydrates. If you want to flavor your coffee, try sprinkling it with cinnamon or cardamom instead—it can even speed up your fat burning process. Just make sure that it doesn't contain any added sugar.
- Keep your diet varied and balanced, with carbohydrates as part of the meal. When you eat carbohydrates together with protein and fat, your GI for the entire meal will be lower. And you won't risk overeating carbohydrates as easily. Usually, when you stuff yourself with sandwiches instead of a cooked meal, you tend to consume a lot more carbs.
- Be cautious about what you drink. A glass of milk may be a good choice with your meal, but think of milk, juice, and similar liquids as part of your meal so that you take into consideration the calories they contain, and their GI value. Quench your thirst with water in between meals.

When Should You Be Eating?

We have already covered the importance of eating four to five smaller meals a day, rather than a few bigger ones. Many people become overweight partially because they don't take the time to plan their meals, and therefore end up eating a lot of semi-processed, processed, and fast foods that are full of calories but low on nutrients. If you skip meals, you will feel hungry and risk eating too much when you do eat. By simply planning your meals for the week, cooking everything from scratch, and using high quality produce, you can help achieve your weight loss goal.

A good day begins with a nice breakfast, and studies show that many people that are overweight tend to skip this important meal. Don't do that. Eat breakfast a little bit later if you have problems eating really early in the morning. You can power walk or bike to your job to work up an appetite, and bring breakfast with you to eat it at work.

When you've just started your exercise regimen, or if you only workout a little bit, you won't need a snack right after your completed workout. You will be just fine with your daily meals.

Index